I0818372

FORAGING FOR HEALING HERBS

How to Find Plants for Charms, Remedies and Rituals

Adele Nozedar

Illustrated by Helen Nicholson

WATKINS
Sharing Wisdom
Since 1893

FORAGING FOR HEALING HERBS
By Adele Nozedar

First published in the UK and USA in 2026 by Watkins,
an imprint of Watkins Media Limited, Unit 11, Shepperton House,
83–89 Shepperton Road, London N1 3DF

enquiries@watkinspublishing.com

Editorial Director: Ella Chappell
Commissioning Editor: Sophie Blackman
Managing Editor: Brittany Willis
Head of Design: Karen Smith
Commissioned Artwork: Helen Nicholson
Production: Uzma Taj

Typeset in Brother 1816
Printed and bound in China

The manufacturer's authorised representative in the EU for product safety is: eucomply OÜ - Pärnu mnt 139b-14, 11317 Tallinn, Estonia, hello@eucompliancepartner.com, www.eucompliancepartner.com

A CIP record for this book is available from the British Library

ISBN: 978-1-83681-021-6 (Hardback)
ISBN: 978-1-83681-038-4 (eBook)

10 9 8 7 6 5 4 3 2 1

www.watkinspublishing.com

CONTENTS

Safety and Sustainability

Before we jump into our foraging adventure, a few housekeeping rules. Without wanting anyone to panic, we need to be aware that some plants are deadly toxic. Some of the most common of these are lords-and-ladies (*Arum maculatum*, see page 140), hemlock water dropwort (*Oenanthe crocata*, see page 156), hemlock (*Conium maculatum*, known as poison hemlock in the USA) and deadly nightshade (*Atropa belladonna*). Other even more frequently encountered dangers plant-wise include foxglove (*Digitalis purpurea*), giant hogweed (*Heracleum mantegazzianum*), daffodils (*Narcissus*) and many more.

Please do not consume any wild plant unless you are absolutely certain of its identification and safety. Carry a pair of gloves in your pocket and use them to handle plants that you don't know. Remember that this book is for information and entertainment purposes only; it is not an identification guide or a medical herbalism manual. Don't rely on apps, either. If you're a complete beginner, your best bet is to learn the ropes by going out with a professional forager. And while it's great to have children that want to be outside, don't let them forage without the guidance of a grown-up.

If you are pregnant or breastfeeding, be extra-cautious as some herbs may cause uterine contractions or be otherwise contra-indicated. In many cases, the impact of plants during pregnancy is simply not known, so better to avoid them.

If you have a health issue of any sort, the advice is always to consult a medical professional before attempting to self-medicate.

In terms of tasting safe wild food, try only a little at first to make sure that there won't be any unexpected allergies. Proceed as you would with any "normal" food that you may not have tried before. If you know you are allergic to any types of food, check medical advice before eating anything you forage. Be aware that some wild foods which are safe to consume in small quantities may cause an adverse reaction in very large amounts; similarly, some plants are good to eat at certain times of year (for example, when the leaves are young) but not others; and it may be that some parts are inedible or need to be cooked before consuming.

We have included a few safety notes through the book to flag up the potential problems of some specific plants, but this information is not comprehensive, and not having a safety note doesn't mean the plant is safe for you to use; for example, your own health situation may make some "edible" plants unsafe for you. Seek medical advice if in any doubt.

Be aware also of potential contaminants, such as run-off from farmland or storm overflows from sewers, either on land or in the sea, or other dangers. If in doubt, forage elsewhere.

In addition to protecting ourselves, we foragers also need to look out for the local wildlife and the plants themselves. Please take no more of the plant than you will consume yourself and only forage where the plant is in abundance. Don't damage the plant or uproot it (in the UK uprooting is actually illegal without permission of the landowner), and make sure you leave plenty of leaves, flowers and seeds behind. Don't take any wild plant without knowing what it is; apart from the danger of being poisonous, it might be rare and protected. Check local restrictions and seek permission to forage. Be aware that even our most common herbs can dwindle away; modern farming practices, such as spraying herbicides, have had a cataclysmic effect on plant diversity, and foragers do not want to make this worse.

Now that has all been said, let's get down to business!

Introduction

Hello! I'm Adele, I'm a forager, and this, unsurprisingly, is a book about plants and foraging. However, this is not your usual plant ID book (although there will be lots of that sort of thing). I might even suggest that this is not like any other foraging book you have ever known.

The best way to describe this book is to regard it as a sort of a quest, in which we embark on an epic journey to find plants that can heal us, soothe us, make us whole and happy in our lives. The quest, with the help of these plants, is to discover what good health really means.

> **Question:** *Do you sometimes feel that this world is becoming a faster one? Possibly . . . too fast?*

Many of us seem to career along at breakneck speed, our genius devices becoming our masters, leaving us worn out and breathless. We have multiple ways of connecting and communicating, but in the midst of all this, we sometimes forget what we wanted to say in the first place. According to Johns Hopkins Medicine, some 38 billion people on this planet are addicted to phones. The use of these devices, they say, reinforces the dopamine pathways that deliver this "feel-good" chemical, in turn reinforcing our reward-seeking behaviour. When the pathways are not reinforced, we experience chemical withdrawal.

Is this you? It's definitely me.

This book seeks a world that is slower; it looks to bypass those frenzied dopamine hits for something more considered, humane, thoughtful, sensory, engaging and interesting . . . and unexpected.

At this point, I need to come clean with you. This book came about in large part because of my own health. Having been as fit as a fiddle for all my life, I had a routine check that showed a shockingly large cancerous growth. All is well now, but in the meantime I had the opportunity to look at things differently, and the time to think about what good health really means.

During my illness, I learned about the Nine Plants Spell, which as you'll see is the starting point of this book. I also found an intriguing stone carving in the local church, just a few minutes from home, that turned out to be quite a rarity: an image of a man from the 10th or 11th century. I kept thinking about what life would have been like for the people of that era, who lived so much closer to nature than we do. Did they use the Nine Plants Spell? What other healing herbs were part of their lives? What would they think of the way we live now? Until I started talking about this being to people in the local church, no one seemed to have noticed him, so I felt that he and I had a personal connection, and that his cute little animated stone face was cheering me on in my quest to find out more about plants and their healing potential.

What did good health mean to the people who carved that stone figure a thousand years ago? There are so many different approaches to healing and some of them are very old, such as Traditional Chinese Medicine or the Ayurvedic system of India, both of which have been around for at least 2,000 years, and very likely more. Western herbal medicine also has a long history, equally ancient, influenced by the Egyptians and physicians of the Middle East. You might have heard of Hippocrates (*c.*460–*c.*370 BCE), whose name is synonymous with healing and who is called the "Father of Medicine". Fundamental to all these healing traditions throughout the globe is the use of plants, in one way or another.

The notion of what constitutes "healing", too, is not as simple as you might imagine. It's not just about being physically and mentally healthy (although that's obviously important), but also encompasses spiritual concepts, including questioning what life really is, and what death is, too. I try to explore this aspect of health in the book, by looking at some of the traditional use of plants in rituals from birth to death, in telling stories of supernatural beings and other realms that exist in tandem to our own, and in general in helping us to understand our place in the eternally mysterious universe. I wonder, too, whether the renaissance of folklore might be due to us yearning to live in simpler, more visceral ways, taking note of the seasons and our part in them, reacting to a need for simplicity in an otherwise chaotic world.

But this is all getting a bit serious!

Plants have stories to tell as well as mysteries to ponder. Throughout this book, you will find out how plant names of all kinds – folk ones, as well as the often unexpectedly poetic botanical names used by Linnaeus – came about. But first, we need to talk about the Nine Plants Spell.

In the 10th century, a physician would use all manner of remedies, many including plants. Whether or not these remedies were generally written down, we don't know. But some of them were and have been preserved for over a thousand years in a manuscript known as the Lacnunga, now safe under glass in the protection of the British Library in London. Compiled in the 10th or 11th century, this manuscript, which offers a fascinating insight into some of the medical practices of the Anglo-Saxons, is a treasure. It includes the Nine Plants Spell, a galdor or healing charm written in Old English which features nine special plants, all of which are still with us today and just as relevant now as they were then.

When I first finished reading about these nine plants, it struck me not only that we might benefit from their healing qualities in our modern world, but also that there are many other herbs that are incredibly useful to us, not just for mysterious magical reasons but for practical ones, too.

So I decided to investigate more healing plants, playing with the idea of the original Nine Plants Spell. To end up with nine times nine (a pleasing and mystical number), I added a further eight sets of nine plants and trees, categorized loosely into their habitats, and describing

some of their healing benefits, as well as a smattering of folklore and some personal stories. I've always had a thing about the mysterious Number Nine, in good company with The Beatles, Norse mythology, and, of course, cats.

Interest in foraging has widened considerably from the pioneering books of Richard Mabey in the 1970s (his *Food for Free* is a classic, a must-buy) to where we are now. Lockdown was an impetus for many, giving people the time to look again at the natural world. Increasing public knowledge about the climate crisis, pollution and loss of species is another flame that has reignited our passion for connecting to nature, alongside concern about the obesity and anxiety associated with our sedentary, urban lives and unhealthy diet. And you might imagine, with all the clever tech that now threatens to replace us human beings, that perhaps we need more than ever to remember who and what we are.

If you're human, you're a forager. Sometimes we forget this. Along with my other foraging friends, I love nothing more than to introduce people to plants, herbs, trees and the like, all of us sharing this beautiful planet. Without plants, we wouldn't survive. By producing oxygen and food, plants are responsible for life on Earth. They also give us medicine, shade on a hot day and shelter when it's cold, and many other practical benefits besides. Their colours and scents delight us, and their stories fascinate us; they make us feel relaxed, refreshed, joyful and uplifted. They were here way before us, and they will be here long after we have disappeared. I find this a comforting thought.

If you look closely at a plant – any plant – have a chat or a long observation with it, sniff its scent and really get to know it as much as any mere human can understand, then you might get the sense that this small and unassuming herb has hidden powers. And you would be right.

CHAPTER 1
THE NINE PLANTS SPELL

The Nine Plants Spell

It is with the Nine Plants Spell that our foraging journey begins. The nine healing herbs discussed are mugwort (*Artemisia vulgaris*), greater plantain (*Plantago major*), shepherd's purse (*Capsella bursa-pastoris*), wood betony (*Betonica officinalis*), chamomile (*Matricaria recutita*), nettle (*Urtica dioica*), crab apple (*Malus sylvestris*), chervil (*Anthriscus cerefolium*) and fennel (*Foeniculum vulgare*). There is some debate about the identity of one or two of the names in the Old English text, but these are the herbs I've chosen to go with, in the interests of simplicity and availability. My source is the wonderful *The Nine Plants Spell* (Hyldyr, 2024), translated by J.S. Hopkins, introduced by Danielle Cudmore and illustrated by Rim Baudey, Anneke Wilder and Jacqui Alberts Lund. I have followed J.S. Hopkins' lead in calling it the Nine Plants Spell, as opposed to the more commonly used Nine Herbs Charm – partly because "plants" is a much broader category than "herbs". All lines quoted from the spell come from this text, with kind permission of the author.

This ancient spell, designed to be chanted as an incantation, seems baffling to 21st-century readers and perhaps was designed to be enigmatic even to its contemporary audience. It invokes Woden (Odin) and the magical and therapeutic powers of the nine plants in order to heal wounds, counter infection and perhaps deal with issues such as insect infestation ("the horror who stalks the land", which sounds demonic, may refer to midges).

The spell goes through the herbs one by one, describing their healing properties, and then gives instructions for combining the ingredients for use as part of a healing spell:

> *"Prepare and apply the salve: Work these plants to dust, and mix them with apple mush. Make a paste of water and ashes. Take Fennel and mix the plant into the boiling paste. Bathe the wound with an egg mixture both before the patient applies the salve and after."*

The words of the galdor are then to be sung multiple times: over each of the plants; then three times before the salve is applied; then three times over the apple; and then into the patient's mouth, into both ears and finally into the wound. (After all that singing you would definitely have the words by heart!)

The point is that *all* these nine plants, clearly considered very special and potent in Anglo-Saxon times, are available and relatively easy to find and use today. You can use the plants in any way you like, individually or together. That is the beauty of combining foraging with folklore.

The most magical of all herbs, mugwort, now steps forward to open the story.

1. Mugwort

(Artemisia vulgaris)

Of all the plants in this curious spell, mugwort was numero uno or rather Una – the first one to be called upon as "Una, that most ancient plant". Addressing mugwort directly, the writer of the spell says,

> *"you defeat venom, you defeat air-illness; you defeat the horror who stalks the land."*

For me, the very prosaic-sounding name "mugwort" didn't seem to live up to the plant's enduring mystery and magic. A book or app won't tell you half of a plant's story; for example, what it smells like or how it feels to touch, its unique personality and that all-important connection between human nature and vegetable nature. I needed to meet mugwort in person. I knew that it liked to be close to water, so one free morning I drove some 40km (25 miles) to a place where I'd heard that mugwort might be found.

After parking the car, I strolled for some time through the meadows and along the riverbank but couldn't see any particularly interesting plants. It was a lovely early September day and there was a bench. As I sat there, gazing into nothing very much, something shifted. The wind started to gust dramatically and a patch of generic greenery – nettles and docks and desiccated brown cleavers – suddenly revealed an underside of glimmering, silvery foliage in among the darker green!

And there was mugwort. Sometimes we can't see what's under our noses.

Here's a quick story for you. Once upon a time, I was part of a little record label, and had to go to the odd black-tie event. These occasions were never my thing, but this was a big one as one of our artists was getting a prize. The venue was in a fancy hotel in Belgravia, with butlers and champagne fountains, and lots of people shouting over each other. Suddenly, a hush swept through the room; someone important was coming. It was Cher. I'd never seen anyone quite so otherworldly. She carried herself like an

Egyptian queen, more regal than any of the other celebrity guests. We were all beglamoured by her presence. And do you know what? That wild, wonderful stand of mugwort instantly reminded me of Cher: a superstar, magical,

mysterious and untameable. I hadn't thought about Cher for years, but here she was, in the form of a weed. And I would never again think of mugwort as sounding awkward or ungainly.

Artemisia vulgaris has many names: apple pie, fellon herb, bulwand, green ginger, sailor's tobacco, fleabane. Then there are all the names for the different species. For example, *Artemesia absinthium*, or wormwood, is used to make absinthe, the preferred tipple of Picasso, Degas and Van Gogh, who all painted pictures of the drink. Mugwort grows all over the planet, with Chinese, Japanese and Norwegian species, plus many more.

HOW TO IDENTIFY MUGWORT

Growing to a height of 1.8m (6ft) and at its best in August, mugwort is often seen by riverbanks, but given a chance will grow anywhere – central reservations of motorways, wasteland, gardens. Rub the herb between your fingers to release the aroma; it's a little like sage! The stems are also aromatic. If you try to pluck the older stems, you will probably fail as they are incredibly tough, so take a knife if you are harvesting. The leaves shift in shape and colour; younger, smaller, darker leaves grow toward the top of the stems, and older leaves are paler and larger. The leaves are deeply cut and shapely, with silvery, slightly fuzzy undersides. The stems grow from green to purple/red. The abundant flowers are brown, red or purplish.

SAFETY: **Avoid mugwort during pregnancy and breastfeeding. Mugwort tea in large doses can be toxic, and there may be other toxic reactions due to the neurotoxin thujone. As with all untested herbs, proceed with caution.**

ALL ABOUT MUGWORT

The insecticidal qualities of mugwort are mentioned in the Nine Plants Spell. A further use is moxibustion, which comes from Chinese medicine. It involves burning a cone or stick of powdered mugwort leaves close to various meridians (energy pathways) and acupuncture points in the body, in order to stimulate the flow of energy.

In some cultures the leaves are used as a flavouring, or to cut through fatty foods. In North America, Indigenous Peoples used mugwort for colds and fevers, and for easing sores, bruises and itching.

Mugwort makes a tea that actually tastes of something, unlike many other herbs. One of the folk names for mugwort is dreamweed. I call mugwort "the yoga dreamer". In Hinduism, the third eye or ajna chakra is situated between the eyebrows and linked with the pineal gland in the brain. It is said to be the gateway to intuition, spirituality and higher consciousness.And among other talents, mugwort can give us access to these realms via the mechanism of lucid dreaming.

I live near a town that has a garrison of British and Gurkha soldiers. A few years back, I was asked by the regiment to take out a foraging group of Welsh, English and Nepalese soldiers. Toward the end of the day one of the Gurkha soldiers remembered that an older retired gentleman who lived in the barracks grew some tall plants. Was it possible for me to visit the garden to see if I knew the name of the plant in English?

It was mugwort, inevitably. I wasn't asked to come into the house as the Mrs wasn't home, but the younger Gurkhas told me the retired soldier used the plant for religious purposes. Parts of it were left on their shrine and parts were used to make kumkum powder, which in Hindu ritual is smudged between the eyebrows on the third eye. I discovered that the Nepalese name for mugwort is *tite pati*. This means "bitter leaf plant", although, personally, I don't find mugwort particularly bitter. I didn't ask if the old soldier used *tite pati* in lucid dreaming, though.

(And yes, I have had a mugwort dream. It's fascinating, although I'm not sure you'd want to do it regularly.)

Chloé's Mugwort Focaccia with a Rock Samphire Garnish

You will need:

500g/1lb 2oz strong white flour
1 x 7g/¼oz sachet dried yeast
2 tsp fine salt
1½ handfuls of mugwort seeds
400ml/14fl oz/1⅔ cups warm water
5 tbsp olive oil, plus extra for greasing and to serve
3 handfuls of fresh rock samphire tips
Flaky sea salt, for sprinkling

1. Tip the flour into a large mixing bowl. Mix the yeast and the salt into the bowl.

2. Add the mugwort seeds, removing the stems by pinching your fingers at the base of each stem.

3. Make a well in the middle of the flour. Add 2 tablespoons of the oil and some warm water, adding the water gradually until you have a sticky dough.

4. Sprinkle the work surface with flour and tip the dough onto it, scraping it from the bowl. Knead for 10–15 minutes until the dough is less sticky. Put it into a clean bowl, cover with a tea towel and leave to prove for 1 hour, or until doubled in size.

5. Oil a shallow rectangular baking pan, measuring roughly 24 x 35cm/9½ x 14in. Tip in the dough and spread it out with your hands to cover the base. Cover with a damp tea towel and leave to rise again for about 20 minutes while you preheat the oven to 220°C/200°C fan/425°F/Gas 7.

6. Wash the rock samphire tips and pat dry with a clean cloth. Once the dough has proved, arrange the sprigs evenly over the surface of the dough.

7. Dimple the dough with your fingertips, so that the samphire sprigs are embedded but visible. Drizzle with the remaining oil, ensuring all samphire sprigs are well covered (use a brush if you need), and 1 tablespoon of water. Sprinkle with flaky salt.

8. Bake for 20 minutes, until golden and risen. While the bread is still hot, drizzle over another 1–2 tablespoons olive oil. Cut into squares and serve either warm or cold, dipping in extra olive oil or picking the samphire while no one is watching!

2. Plantain

(Plantago spp.)

The second ingredient in the Nine Plants Spell is "Waybread, plant-mother", which is greater plantain (*Plantago major*). I will also look at the similar ribwort plantain (*Plantago lanceolata*), which in medieval days was called "ribs" (from the "ribby" appearance of its leaves). There are some 250 species of plantain on the planet. As is often the case, the most useful plants are the ones that are so common that we can't see them.

HOW TO IDENTIFY PLANTAIN

As mentioned in the spell itself, greater plantain just loves compacted soil, trampled by passing wheels and feet:

> *"Carts creaked over you, women rode over you, over you brides bellowed, over you bulls snorted!"*

The leaves, which grow in a rosette and can be seen for most of the year, are strong and broad, with distinctive veins that run through the leaf and curve around the edges. The mature plant sends out small, straw-coloured flower spikes that can grow to 40cm (16in), shedding edible seeds to make more plants. If left to grow, greater plantain, with its impressive flower spike, is worthy of being put into a beautiful pot for all to admire. Ribwort plantain is similar looking but with narrower leaves, and flowerheads on the top of stems.

ALL ABOUT GREATER PLANTAIN

Although plantain is often thought of as a weed, we foragers see things differently. Weeds are often the most useful, powerful and accessible plants, and so we might as well claim that word "weed" as a symbol of power. The plantain was honoured as the "plant-mother" for good reason. When crushed, plantain (of both kinds) is a styptic; that is, a plant that can be used to staunch the flow of blood. This tends to be more effective in greater plantain, possibly because the leaves are larger. Both kinds of plantain are used in herbalism for their healing powers, including antimicrobial and anti-inflammatory properties, in cases of mild bronchitis, cystitis, catarrh, ear infections and more. Ribwort plantain is used for lung infections, helping the respiratory tract to heal. For diarrhoea, the

tannin content in plantain leaves, when taken as a strong tea, is said to be effective. Other uses of plantains include reducing mouth ulcers, toothache, gum disease and tonsillitis.

Plantains are full of various vitamins and minerals and, because there are no known contraindications, are very safe, even during pregnancy and for use with children. The seeds are edible, too, used in the same way as psyllium husks (dietary fibre from the seeds of *Plantago*) and with the same mucilaginous (gelatinous) properties, so are sometimes used as in recipes in which a thickening agent is called for.

When the Nine Plants Spell was first created, it is unlikely that the Native American peoples would have known plantain. When the European settlers arrived, however, they brought some stowaways with them. Seeds of both kinds of plantain, tiny enough to be unnoticed, hopped on board the ships, settling themselves into pockets, hats, baggage and, of course, boots. The Indigenous Peoples quickly gave the plant a name: white man's footprint. The Cree people in Canada called it *mahkipakiw*, meaning "weed". The German Catholic priest Sebastian Kneipp (1821–97), one of the founding fathers of the naturopathic movement, said "the plantain seals open wounds as if sewn with a gold thread", a wonderfully lyrical description.

The plant, evidently, settles in nicely wherever it goes. It's highly likely that, if you were to step away from this book and go outside, right now, you would find it.

When I was a kid, it emerged that I was terrible at field sports. I would be sent to the furthest part of the pitch, in a well-meaning bid by the sports teacher to make sure that I was unlikely to even see the ball, let alone touch it. That's where I found out about plantain. In the spirit of exploration and avoiding the ball, I discovered that you could make a whistle of the leaves, as well as play a game called "guns" by wrapping the stem around the flowerhead and shooting it off into the air (the lanceolate kind is best for this last use).

Using cleaned greater plantain leaves (in, say, a risotto) mimics both the flavour and scent of fungi. Just pop the leaves on the top of the cooked dish, cover for 15 minutes or so, remove and serve. It's really yummy (that is, if you like the taste of mushrooms). Ribwort plantain tends to be "wetter" and not so flavoursome.

Soft Hands and a Smell Test

There are a couple of further uses for greater plantain, too.

1. Find a couple of cleanish plantain leaves, then roll the leaves between your hands until damp.

2. Drop the leaves and wave your hands in the air until dry. Now feel your hands. They will feel soft. This is why various high-end cosmetics companies use the plant as a skin conditioner.

3. Now find another couple of leaves, roll and fold the leaves again, but this time, have a really good sniff.

4. What can you smell? Most of you will have a vague idea of a scent but will be unable to pinpoint it. However, usually in a group of 20 foragers there will be one who says "mushroom" straightaway, without thinking. It takes just that one person, then there are "oohs!" and "ahs!" as everyone else gets it. This little game can discern if someone has a better than average sense of smell, and I do think that is a kind of superpower.

3. Shepherd's Purse

(Capsella bursa-pastoris)

For its third ingredient, the Nine Plants Spell records lamb's cress as well as two names, *stune* and *stithe*, one of which may refer to shepherd's purse, "She who grows on stone". Given the age of the spell and the possibility that several people may have contributed to the text, I thought it was best to keep things simple and stick with shepherd's purse. *Bursa* means "bag" in Latin, *capsula* means a "small box or capsule" and *pastoris* is a "shepherd", hence shepherd's purse. Although traditionally a shepherd's purse would have been made from the scrotum of a goat!

HOW TO IDENTIFY SHEPHERD'S PURSE

You will find shepherd's purse on cultivated and disturbed ground in many parts of the world, where it has naturalized freely. Shepherd's purse is a brassica. It can be distinguished from other family members by its heart-shaped seedpods, a really beautiful example of nature's technological genius. Its stem grows to a range of heights (from 2cm/¾in to 70cm/28in) from a rosette of lobed leaves. The small, white flowers and the heart-shaped seeds can appear at any time of year.

***SAFETY:* Avoid shepherd's purse during pregnancy or if you have thyroid or heart problems.**

ALL ABOUT SHEPHERD'S PURSE

I am always impressed by those herbs that are able to travel everywhere, welcome refugees that we all know and think belong to us, but are at home throughout the entire planet. In this case, shepherd's purse can be traced back to the ancient city of Çatalhöyük (in modern-day Turkey), meaning that it has a shared history with humans going back almost 10,000 years.

As with many "weeds", shepherd's purse is handy because of its ability to survive very harsh temperatures. The seeds survive for a long time in the soil until needed, waiting for up to 30 years, and one plant is able to produce some 64,000 seeds. It is said that this plant is the second-most prolific weed in the world. (This begs the question: which is the first? The answer might be prostrate knotweed (*Polygonum aviculare*). Although this knotweed does not thrive in the Arctic, anywhere else, it seems, is fair game for this energetic little plant.)

If you have ever reached for mustard to add some heat to a meal, that flavour is that of a brassica. In medieval England, the plant family was nicknamed "salt and pepper". The root of shepherd's purse can be used as a substitute for ginger and for salt (see recipe opposite), while the leaves are tasty and nutritious, good mixed in with dandelion leaves and chicory.

Young shepherd's purse plants were once sold in the markets of New York in the springtime. On the other side of the world, the Japanese use it as an essential ingredient in a ceremonial barley-rice porridge made for the Festival of Seven Herbs, aka Nanakusa-no-sekku, which takes place on 7 January. The idea is that the broth, featuring seven herbs, will bring longevity and health and ward off evil during a time of year when there's not much of nutritional value about. As well as shepherd's purse, the other ingredients are Japanese parsley, cudweed, chickweed, nipplewort, turnip and radish.

Shepherd's purse is also medicinal. A tea made from the plant is described by several sources as a "sovereign remedy" against haemorrhages, in particular of the kidneys, and serious bruising. In World War II, German soldiers relied on an extract of the herb as a topical treatment for wounds when there was very little else to do the job.

There are many more interesting facts about this plant, but I recently discovered something that was so unexpected that it eclipses everything else. It seems that shepherd's purse is not quite as innocent as we might suppose, and has an unusual adaptation known as myxospermy. When the plant is made moist by the soil, the seeds exude a sweet, mucilaginous "thing" that traps, and then digests, small insects and minuscule microorganisms. As a seed grows and eventually germinates, the nutrients from the insects are absorbed, feeding the seedling. This means that shepherd's purse is protocarnivorous. Usually, carnivorous plants (think venus fly traps, pitcher plants and sundews), which have evolved to ingest insects, prefer to live in boggy conditions. But shepherd's purse grows in gardens, fields, wastelands and the like. So far, scientists don't know the reason why shepherd's purse should be any different. Fascinating!

Shepherd's Purse Salt Substitute

This recipe is very simple, but finding the ingredients might be harder than you think.

It's fine to dry the ingredients you have and store them while you find the rest. Combine more or less equal amounts of dried shepherd's purse leaves and seeds, wild mint, young tansy leaves, nettle leaves, lambs' quarter leaves, goldenrod leaves, yellow dock leaves, juniper berries and wild carrot leaves. Blend them together in a clean coffee grinder (or similar) and sift the resulting powder through fine sieve. Make lots as it's really good, if a tad time consuming, but all foragers like something for free (and I also suspect that we like projects that can take time!).

4. Wood Betony

(Betonica officinalis)

The fourth ingredient in the Nine Plants Spell is "Venom-Loathe", which is probably wood betony or betony (both names refer to the same plant). According to the Roman naturalist Pliny, the name comes from the Vettones, a pre-Roman Iberian tribe of the third century BCE, who discovered it. A further idea suggests that it might derive from an amalgam of two Celtic words: *bew* for "head" and *ton* (to improve).

HOW TO IDENTIFY WOOD BETONY

A member of the dead nettle family (*Lamiaceae*, also known as the mint family), along with plants such as sage, lavender, oregano and basil, betony does not have a pungent scent. It looks a little like self-heal (*Prunella vulgaris*), but the dainty "wings" that stick out from the stem below the flower spike are a giveaway. The pink-purple flower spikes typically grow to 30cm (12in), but the plant can reach twice that height.

Betony can be found between June and October, depending on where you live. If you locate it, make a note of where, as it is a perennial. Betony will live in open grassland but seems to be happier tucked a little way underneath overhanging verges, at least in my experience.

ALL ABOUT BETONY

In Italian, there are two sayings: "May you have more virtues than betony" and "Sell your coat and buy betony". One of the magical uses of this plant is for purification and protection. It was believed that betony protected not only the body, but also the soul. If placed beneath a pillow, it is said to shield you from visions and dreams.

Betony was also cultivated in monasteries, convents and graveyards to keep away evil. It was traditional to burn the plant on a bonfire and then jump through the smoke at midsummer for purification and protection. Personally, I feel that burning is unkind to the plant, but scattering a few flowers along doorways and windows to protect your home seems like a good idea. In addition, there's an interesting rumour that the plant can prevent intoxication.

The notion of protection takes many guises, some more "real" than others, but all equally important. Good health is seated in the body, the mind and also in the spirit (or whatever you prefer to call it). In 1526, *The Grete Herball* suggested combining betony with wine "for them that ben to ferfull", and betony is still renowned as a tonic for the nervous system. As a tea it is calming, soothing and helpful to release tensions. For people who are troubled, nervous or unable to sleep, a cup of betony tea – bright green and relaxing – might be just what is needed. Not so long ago, betony was used as a sedative for madness, and it is still called upon for anxiety and fearfulness.

Betony helps memory, recollection, grounding and feeling safe. It is associated with the solar plexus region – the gut, belly or stomach. In yoga, this is the site of the manipura chakra, which, if in balance, promotes confidence and self-esteem. It is this area of the body that is often overridden by our busy heads. If you are nervous or anxious, try centring yourself by touching your solar plexus, and remembering to breathe!

Experience has shown me that this powerful herb might be in danger. Recently, I set out to find some betony in the wild. Where I saw the plant a few years ago, there had been quite a nice stand. This time, nothing. So I searched further afield. Nothing. On day three, I found 20 perfect specimens. As betony stems are tough and I didn't have a knife, I decided to harvest the next day. But when I returned I was shocked to see that a verge clearer had come through and smashed the lot, leaving smatterings of dead purple mess. I now grow betony in my garden.

5. Chamomile

(Matricaria recutita)

Here comes the fifth ingredient of the Nine Plants Spell. This herb's achievement, we learn, which is said to have taken place "at Alorford", is,

> *"that no one should lose their life to disease, since for him Chamomile was prepared."*

There are at least two plants called chamomile that could be used: German chamomile (*Matricaria recutita*) and Roman chamomile (*Chamaemelum nobile*). Those of you who know your plants will notice that it is German chamomile that I've highlighted in this section. The Roman variety, whose original home was in northern Africa, tends to be less hardy than the German kind, and in addition is said to be more prone to triggering allergies as an essential oil. The issue is not the raw chamomile itself but the essential oil used with Roman chamomile.

HOW TO IDENTIFY CHAMOMILE

Let's start with German chamomile. It looks like a large daisy on a tall stem with narrow, branched leaves. The white petals are arched back, meaning that bees and other insects have easy access to the yellow flowers. The plant can grow up to 50cm (20in) tall. If in doubt, find a knife and cut the flower base; it will be hollow on the inside. Also called scented mayweed, this is the kind of chamomile that is most often made into the popular tea. The scent is distinctive, rather lovely, and shared by both types.

Roman chamomile looks very similar indeed, but unlike the other, it is perennial, meaning that it grows every year. It is considerably smaller than the German type, between 15–30cm (6–12in) tall. And if you have the inclination to make a lawn of the plant, this is the one to find.

The Nine Plants Spell asks chamomile to remember what it achieved at Alorford, meaning "Alderford", which might sound like a place name, but it might just refer to a more general type of environment. Alder the tree likes to hang out in marshy places, such as bogs. And so does chamomile, although it can also be found in grasslands, along field edges and in gardens and parks.

ALL ABOUT CHAMOMILE

The Norse tribes believed chamomile to be sacred. Because of its sunny yellow colour, they dedicated the little plant to the sun god Baldur, the son of Odin and the goddess Frigg. They called the plant "Baldur's eyebrows". It's charming to think that the rudimentary sun pictures, drawn in crayons by children, share the same idea. The name chamomile comes from two words in Greek: *kamai* (earth) and *melon* (apple), as the plant not only grows in the earth but is scented very much like an apple. The name of the light sherry Manzanilla was inspired by the chamomile. The Egyptians, too, revered the herb. They also dedicated it to the sun (no surprises there) and used it for its magical properties as well as its healing ones.

One German name for chamomile translates as "can do anything", and a Scottish legend tells us that "a cup of chamomile tea will do more than three doctors". Chamomile is drunk by millions of people around the planet, so let's dig a little deeper into why that cup of tea is so soothing.

The plant is antifungal, antibacterial, anti-inflammatory, antiseptic and antispasmodic. Notably, it is a useful and unharmful sedative. It counters urinary tract infections, can calm lactating mothers and their babies, and also helps breastfeeding mothers to produce milk. It's well known for relieving menstrual cramping too – the *matricaria* part of German chamomile's name derives from the Latin *matrix*, meaning "womb", or *mater*, "mother". *The Good Housewife's Handbook*, dated 1500, offers the following:

"A fine oil of chamomile can be prepared when one takes olive oil and adds chamomile flowers; the more flowers, the stronger it becomes."

After infusing for 4–6 weeks in the sun (such as on a windowsill), strain the liquid through fine muslin. It then has a variety of uses, including easing colic in children, cystitis, constipation and more.

There's another old Scottish saying that goes "to comfort the brain, smell chamomile".

Chamomile Steam Bath

Used in cases of colds and flu as well as asthma, a chamomile steam bath will not only lessen a fever but will also calm the patient, enabling a good night's sleep. It's worth gathering the herb as you find it during the summer months and drying it before the winter.

As with a lavender bag, enclose the chamomile in some linen or other loose-weave fabric then sew it up. Simply run the bath with the bag hanging in the warm flowing water. There's something motherly and soothing about the plant; the name says it all.

6. Nettle

(Urtica dioica)

Nettle is the sixth ingredient in the Nine Plants Spell. Quite a few plants look "nettly"; for example, lemon balm, dead nettles, hemp nettles. But here we are looking at the common or garden nettle (*Urtica dioica*), also known as Devil's wort, presumably for its habit of stinging anyone who gets close. However, nettle's health-giving properties are recognized in this old English saying:

> *"If they'd eat nettles in*
> *March, And mugwort in May*
> *So many fine maidens,*
> *Wouldn't go to the clay."*

So far, our search for the nine plants seems to have been among the commonest of plants. Nettle is no exception. There are nettle species in all parts of the world, from New Zealand to Hawaii to China to the Himalayas, far too many to name – a testament to this plant's versatility.

HOW TO IDENTIFY NETTLE

The Latin name *urtica* means "sting". Often, we find nettles by the simple accident of brushing against them, usually in summer with bare legs and flimsy footwear! Otherwise, look for the hairs along the stem and tooth-like leaves, with the plants growing up to 1m/3¼ft or possibly more. If you are planning to eat nettle, gather young plants in early spring, before the yellowish-green, catkin-like flowers appear. Nettles are found in gardens, fields, hedgerows, woodlands, country lanes and wasteland.

SAFETY: **Nettles can cause a rash. The tried-and-tested way to reduce the pain is rubbing with a dock leaf – bitter dock (*Rumex obtusifolius*) or curled dock (*Rumex crispus*) – but this isn't as effective as the juice of common sorrel (*Rumex acetosa*, see page 226). Otherwise treat with**

calamine. Seek medical advice if the hives persist or if you experience an allergic reaction. If eating nettle, note that between June and October the herb can have a laxative effect as well as possible urinary tract issues.

ALL ABOUT NETTLE

If you ever accidentally use a strimmer on nettles, you will quickly know the error of your ways as the wire becomes taffled up in the strong stems. The uses for these stems include cordage and all manner of woven cloth, with examples surviving from the Bronze Age, still in good condition. In addition, nettle makes two different dyes: the roots give us a yellow dye; the leaves, a pale green one.

As you might guess, a plant of such renown caught the gods' attention. The nettle was dedicated to Thor, god of thunder, fertility and marriage. Pliny advised that the plant was sacred, to be eaten year round (although this may not be the case in practice, see above). There were beliefs about how and when to gather nettles; what were originally pagan restrictions were absorbed into Christianity, with people advised to gather nettles on specific days (Christmas Day, New Year, Easter, Epiphany, etc.). Nettles picked and gathered on Maundy Thursday and eaten as a vegetable were meant to preserve the eater from want of food for the following year.

Nettles, according to a Germanic folk song, were symbols of "fidelity in love". The plant is also believed to be protective. This applies not just to nettles but also to any plants with hairs, thorns or prickles, which were seen as a guard against demons. Very much the plant of the witch, nettles were often used in potions and unguents; crossroads where nettles grew were said to be places where witches gathered.

An unusual way to show deference, and one that might not have stood the test of time, was the Belgian ritual in which people would lash themselves with nettles dipped in urine. And here are two more folkloric practices that don't translate to the modern era. One was to find out if a girl was a virgin. She had to urinate on nettles; if they withered, she was no longer a virgin. However, if a woman's urine withered nettles, then she was barren.

As a food, the nettle, despite its stings, is nutritious and tasty, although the young stems (also the stingiest) are the best. It has been hailed as the most health-giving plant on the planet, packed with vitamins and minerals, including iron, magnesium and calcium (among others). Nettle has been used for hundreds of years to treat painful muscles and joints, eczema, arthritis and gout. It is a flavoursome ingredient in dishes; my particular favourite is horta, a Greek pie that uses handfuls of different and often unnamed leafy green plants of which nettle is the star of the show, along with chunks of feta, seasoned with nutmeg and cooked in a deep pie dish.

A couple of years ago, I had an email from a man in his 30s who wanted his mum to come on a foraging course. He added that she didn't walk very well and so didn't want to be in a group as she was embarrassed. No problem, I said, and almost forgot about them. Then, some time later, the son contacted me again. His mum was much better and was ready to go foraging. She was a nice, smiley lady and, as we walked, I noticed that she occasionally picked nettles, bundling up the stems and gently lashing the leaves across her hands. I knew what she was doing – urtication (from *Urtica*, the name of the plant) – but I'd never seen this in practice, so I asked her who had suggested it. Turns out that it was the son. Studies tell us that the application of stinging nettle reduces inflammation, relieving conditions such as arthritis. The contact of nettle with skin produces a counterirritant, which can override musculoskeletal pain.

When things like this happen, I thank my lucky stars that I do what I do. And there is no doubt that the humble and mighty stinging nettle deserves its place in the Nine Plants Spell.

Nettle Hay Fever Remedy

This is wonderfully effective.
Simply gather a handful of fresh spring stinging nettles, clean under a tap (using rubber gloves) and pop into a teapot with honey to taste. Leave to infuse for 5 minutes, then strain. Drink little and often.

7. Crab apple

(Malus sylvestris)

The seventh ingredient in the Nine Plants Spell is the crab apple, another one that's humble but mighty to add to our foraging repertoire. Of all apples, it's the crab apples that I love the most, the ones that are called *Malus sylvestris*, whose name means "pertaining to the woods" or "growing wild" or "forested". I like them because you never know what you're going to taste, and as a forager that's a rather exciting possibility!

Apples originated in Kazakhstan, and Alma Ata (now known as Almaty), which means "full of apples". Apples love to cross-fertilize, so there are unknown varieties of them, some named, some not. A friend of mine who loves apples has a garden that boasts a fruit that is said to be the first wild apple, *Malus sieversii*, the ancestor of the domestic apple.

HOW TO IDENTIFY CRAB APPLE

Do we really need to know what an apple looks like? Not as crazy as you might think. In fact, the apples in standard supermarkets are very different to the wilder ones. These renegade crab apples are generally smallish, in reds and yellows, dolls' house fruits with a flavour that ranges from edible and tangy to toe-curlingly acidic.

Crab apple trees are often used in gardens as ornamentals, and these are the easiest to find; befriend the owner. In the wild, keep your eyes to the ground in the winter months. The apples often collect around the tree, meaning that you will be able to recognize the blossom and the fruit later in the year. A crab apple can be as small as the bell on a cat's collar.

ALL ABOUT CRAB APPLES

Apples feature prominently in myth and legend. It was the Apple of Discord, which was awarded to the most beautiful woman of all, starting the Trojan War. Then there's the story of Adam and Eve. Famously, Eve colluded with the Devil in serpent form to tempt Adam into eating the fruit of the Tree of Knowledge – assumed to be an apple – causing them to be cast out from the Garden of Eden. The idea of a serpent still holds a frisson of fear for us. Mention of a "wyrm", serpents and venom frequently pop up in the Nine Plants Spell, symbolizing illness.

If you cut an apple in half with the stalk at the top, you will find five pips inside, arranged in a five-pointed star. This pentagram is the basis of the Golden Ratio or the Fibonacci Sequence, which is seen in the natural world in many guises; the beautiful curves of the Nautilus shell are a particularly wonderful example.

The saying "an apple a day keeps the doctor away" is known around the globe in various languages. In Norse mythology, apples were a symbol of immortality, guarded by the goddess Idun, giver of eternal youth. Her task was to store the apples that the gods ate to keep themselves young. Apples are symbolic of death as well as life. Avalon, meaning "Isle of the Apples", is where King Arthur in some versions of the legend goes to die. Merlin, the magician, lives and works in a grove of apples, whose fruits gave him the power of prophecy.

In my opinion, the sour kind of crab apples are the best because they have a high pectin content that makes them ideal for jams and jellies. Ayurvedic medicine uses these apples as a cure for gout, inflammation and constipation; and recently, red crab apples are being looked at by scientists as a possible way of limiting the growth of cancer cells.

Apples play a part in Hallowe'en rituals, of course. If you eat an apple by the light of a Hallowe'en moon, the fruit will give nourishment to the souls of the dead who wander about at that time of year. A few years ago, at Hallowe'en, I accidentally scorched some homemade toffee, so decided to make miniature "cocktail" toffee apples using crab apples. They were delicious, especially if you like slightly burnt toffee.

Crab Apple Cider Vinegar

Although apple cider vinegar can be bought relatively easily, this is an ideal and easy way to use up a glut of apples or pears. Ferments are known to be great for gut health as well as being useful for adding flavour to stocks, recipes that call for a sour flavour, etc. Don't worry about the sugar in the recipe – it will change to alcohol and then into acetic acid, and the end product will contain minimal alcohol or sugar.

You will need:

Apples and pears, chopped (including any scraps, such as the core and peel, which would otherwise be binned)

Sugar (quantity as per method)

A glug of the "Mother", that is, the cloudy substance in the bottom of an old apple cider vinegar bottle

1. Fill a container halfway with chopped apples or pears, then fill with water from a measuring jug so that you can make a note of how much you are adding. Leave a little space at the top.

2. Add sugar in a ratio of 1 tablespoon per 240ml/9fl oz/1 cup water and let dissolve; it's OK to warm on a stovetop if necessary.

3. Add a good glug of the "Mother".

4. Cover your container with cloth, such as a tea towel or old pillowcase, and leave it somewhere dark and warmish. Stir daily for the next 2 weeks.

5. After 2 weeks, strain and pour the liquid into a clean container. Leave, covered with cloth, for a few months. Keep an eye on your vinegar and have a sniff from time to time; when it smells as sharp as a sharp apple, it's done!

6. While you wait for the vinegar, gather, clean and sterilize the screw-top glass bottles you will need to store it in.

7. Once ready, funnel the vinegar into the bottles. Keep in a cool place and use the natural sediment (the "Mother") to make more crab apple vinegar.

Remember that this wonderful ingredient was, not long ago, made in a fairly unmethodical way, and don't worry too much; if you can keep the ingredients in a warmish place you can't go wrong.

8. Chervil

(Anthriscus cerefolium)

Now, we approach the eighth ingredient in the Nine Plants Spell: chervil, sometimes known as French parsley. This plant is often paired with ingredient nine in the spell: "Fille and Fennel, a most mighty pair!", the plants shaped by the "wise lord" himself – Woden (Odin). Chervil, or *Anthriscus cerefolium*, is part of the umbellifer family, so-called because the top of the flower looks rather like an umbrella. Other umbellifers include celery and parsley, as well as some extremely poisonous plants (see below and page 35). Chervil was, at one time, called *myrrhis*. This is because the volatile oil of the plant has a scent very similar to myrrh, the spice mentioned in the Bible.

HOW TO IDENTIFY CHERVIL

There are several kinds of chervil, including wild chervil, which is also known as cow parsley; you may well have noticed the delicate, frothy stems along verges, lanes and trackways in the summer months, followed by the tall, brittle stems as the plant disappears into the autumn and winter. Although wild chervil is edible, in this instance I am reluctant to suggest that you chase after it with the idea of eating it unless you are absolutely certain that you know what it is. This is because chervil is part of the wild carrot family. Although there are edible members (such as Queen Anne's lace, *Daucus carota*), this category also includes some of the most dangerous plants for humans, dogs, cats and cattle, such as hemlock (deadly) and hemlock water dropwort (also deadly). Hemlock is commonly seen in and around water but is often found in other areas too – for example, I recently noticed a large stand of it at the back of a school football pitch. If you would like to taste the liquorice-like leaves of chervil, find it in a reputable garden centre.

SAFETY: **Because of the danger of inadvertently foraging one of the similar-looking extremely toxic plants, I suggest you neither pick nor eat chervil in the wild. You might also find it useful to know that chervil, along with other plants of the Apiaceae family, can cause "strimmer dermatitis" (when human skin reacts to some plants' leaves).**

ALL ABOUT CHERVIL

In terms of medicine, chervil is used as an expectorant and digestive. Both the 1st-century Roman scholar Pliny and the 17th-century herbalist Culpeper believed that it "does much please and warm old stomachs". The herb has, over the years, also been used as a stimulant, a dissolver of congealed blood, and a healer of eczema, gout, kidney stones and menstrual issues.

If there are any gardeners among you, you might like to know that slugs are, apparently, attracted to chervil; it is supposed that the slugs feed on the tasty leaves of the plant, which can be used as a foil to "save" other, more tender plants.

Serious food lovers will know that this herb is one of the four traditional "fine herbs", in company with tarragon (see pages 54–55), chives and parsley (see pages 43–45). These are usually added to the dish at the last moment, as the herbs are so fragrant and delicate; the most lovely part added last. In European folklore, chervil was eaten not only for the flavour and the digestive benefits, but also because the herb "could inspire cheerfulness and sharp wits". Medieval monks cultivated the herb because they believed it had spiritual properties as well as the culinary and medicinal ones.

Try chervil pounded into butter with sea salt, black pepper and lemon juice, to go with a fish dish. Or add the chopped herb to a gazpacho, or use it to spice up scrambled eggs for breakfast.

9. Fennel

(Foeniculum vulgare)

The final ingredient in the Nine Plants Spell is fennel. This originated in and around the Mediterranean basin, but can now be found in most parts of the globe: an ancient, seasonal herb. As well as being cultivated, it is also found in the wild. In addition to this, it is thriving in my own garden in Wales, and those of my neighbours too. One particularly tall plant has plonked itself on a kerbside in the middle of the village; long may its beauty prosper.

Fennel was spread about, like many other culinary herbs, by monks. Its fame was such that it was mentioned in the *Capitulare de Villis*, a complex set of rules and regulations issued by the Carolingian royalty for the governance of their estates. The edict on fennel was that it had to be grown in every one of the many estate gardens.

HOW TO IDENTIFY FENNEL

There are several varieties of fennel to consider. Common fennel (*Foenicium vulgare*) and sweet fennel (*Foeniculum vulgare* var. *dulce*) are both grown for their seeds and leaves; sweet fennel has a milder flavour that common fennel. Florence fennel (also known as bulb fennel, *Foeniculum vulgare* var. *azoricum*) is grown for its bulb. Bronze fennel (*Foeniculum vulgare purpureum*) has a lovely purplish colour.

Sweet fennel will grow to a height of 2m (6½ft), with up to 40 flat "umbels" on one plant. The seeds start out as a tender green and age to a faded grey. If you are a keen gardener, a small packet of seeds should keep you in seeds (and other parts of the plant) for years to come.

I am more of an enthusiastic gardener than a good one, but I find that fennel is one plant that just rolls up its shirtsleeves and grows and grows . . . and grows!

ALL ABOUT FENNEL

Fennel seeds have been used for culinary purposes for 2,000 years and more. It is these seeds, which have a long shelf-life, that you are given at the end of an Indian meal as a digestif. Just in case you didn't know, the name for these sweetened seeds is *mukhwas*. Fennel is also used in some toothpastes for its clean and refreshing taste, and its feathery green leaves add a liquorice flavour to dishes. These days we tend not to use the stems, and this is a shame as they are also delicious and crunchy.

The Greek called fennel *marathon*; the battlefield that gave the long-distance race its name was so-called because of all the fennel plants that grew there. They used fennel to stimulate milk production in breastfeeding mothers, just as we do today. Not quite so useful was the advice that fennel, taken with wine, was an antidote to snakebites.

Because the Roman gladiators used fennel as a stimulant, the most successful fighters were crowned with fennel leaves. In this case, the plant meant "you deserve all praise".

Fennel was considered protective, too. Similar to other plants that contain essential oils (dill, parsley, caraway), it is an anti-demonic remedy. According to some German tales, fennel could drive away dwarfs, which were not always the cute Disney versions that we know and love, but were thought of as much darker beings. In England, fennel was attached to the doors and windows of houses on the night of St John the Baptist (23 June) to ward off any lurking non-human entities. Another way of counteracting the possible dangers of St John's Night in some parts of France and England was

to stuff the keyholes of the house with fennel while reciting a magical spell which went something like this:

"If a wizard tries to enter through this hole tonight, have a good sniff, please, Fennel, and he will get such a fright that he will be afraid to enter."

Some beekeepers would rub crushed fennel onto and inside bee hives so that the bees would stay close to the hives. Bees love the scent of the herb, so this makes sense.

In herbal medicine, fennel is used for some 43 different types of ailments, which range from simple ones (such as coughs, colds and cuts) to more complex issues, including kidney problems and cancer. Perhaps one of the best-known uses of fennel, though, is to do with the mouth; both fruit and seed are used as a mouthwash for gum disorders. For hopeful gentlemen whose hair is thinning, the seed oil of the herb just might help. Worth a try!

On with our quest!

We've reached the end of the magical herbs of the Nine Plants Spell. Do you have some ideas about how to work with these wonderful plants? Now let's see what other combinations of nine herbs we might find in our modern world, starting with – and this might come as a surprise to the foragers among you – the garden!

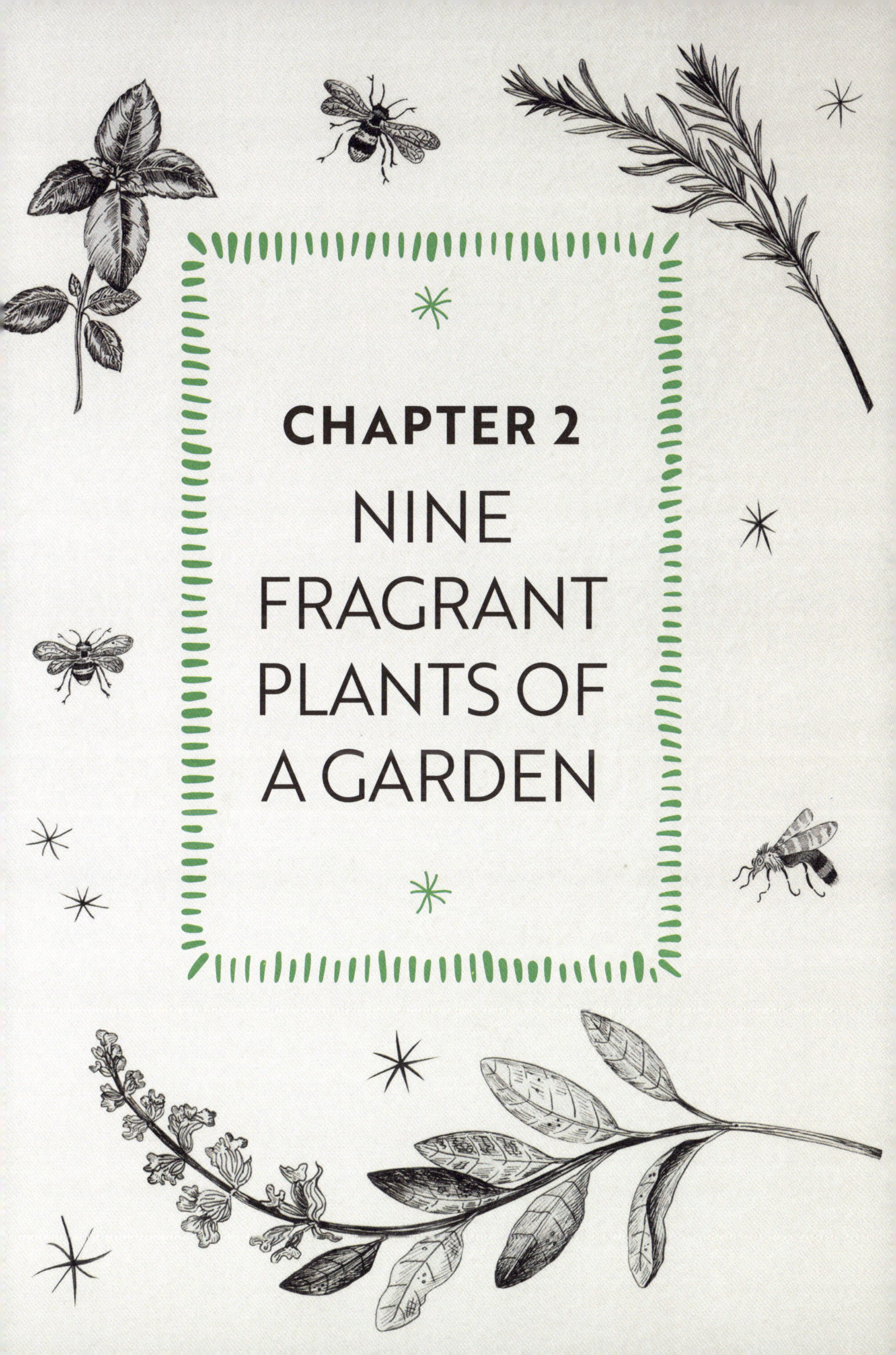

CHAPTER 2

NINE FRAGRANT PLANTS OF A GARDEN

Nine Fragrant Plants of a Garden

You might well raise an eyebrow when you find that the next chapter is about fairly common garden plants and not really what we might think of as "normal" foraging at all.

Once upon a time, however, these plants would have been great foraging material, as well as being thought to be magical; the many stories and folkloric ideas tell us so. Seen in a different light, the herbs in your ordinary weekly shop might suddenly reveal themselves as much more noble beings, the status of deities, yet rudely wrapped in cellophane and scanned at a checkout. (The ignominy!)

When did these mysterious, sacred herbs become the reliable culinary garden staples that they are now? I hope this chapter will help you see them with new eyes.

1. Parsley & 2. Celery

(Petroselinum & Apium graveolens)

Roman writers used the word *apium*, which, it seems, was a sort of catch-all for several herbs of the wild carrot family, including parsley and celery, with the result that the two of them share some folkloric secrets and so are being described together here, although we now use one as a herb and the other as a vegetable.

For our purposes, there are two sorts of parsley. The curled sort is *Petroselinum crispum*, and the flat one, also called Italian parsley, is *Petroselinum crispum neapolitanum*. The latter is the one generally preferred by chefs as it has a slightly stronger taste.

Other tasty delicacies in the wild carrot family include coriander, fennel and dill, but there are also some deadly toxic specimens, such as hemlock and hemlock water dropwort (see page 156). In addition, wild parsnip and other members of the Apiaceae/Umbelliferae family

can be mistaken for something less dangerous. We do not need to eat any of these, so . . . don't!

HOW TO IDENTIFY PARSLEY AND CELERY

Garden parsley, as a cultivated herb, is to be looked for in the supermarket or garden centre rather than in the wild. Celery (*Apium graveolens*), on the other hand, does grow wild, on the coast or in brackish water environments, such as on tidal riverbanks or in marshes, but as with parsley, foraging it for food is not recommended (see safety below). As with other members of the Apiaceae family, the flowers of parsley and celery are clustered in white umbels. Parsley leaves are either curled or flat, and the plant has a distinctive smell. Celery has glossy, dark green leaves, long, crisp stalks and its own recognizable scent.

***SAFETY:* The Apiaceae or wild carrot family (see page 156), which includes parsley and celery, contains some of the most deadly of wild plants; do not eat or touch them unless you are certain of what you are looking at. Apps are not a failsafe.**

ALL ABOUT PARSLEY AND CELERY

Parsley and celery had an important part to play in various death cults. Celery was dedicated to Hades, the Ruler of the Underworld. At that time, celery was not the innocuous crunchy stem beloved of dieters it is today, but instead was eaten at funeral meals and twisted into wreaths for the dead. Both parsley and celery essential oils smell unpleasant, which caused people to think that they would keep away evil spirits (although if I were an evil spirit, I think that I'd be delighted to annoy people with my nasty smells).

In some areas, parsley was once boiled and given to anyone believed to be bewitched, and in Spain a bride would carry bread and parsley to ward off evil spirits. Parsley was also used to fill in the cracks and joints in pigsties to protect the animals from being hexed (signs of which would include the animal not eating, for example). Parsley is also known for taking a long time to germinate; the seeds apparently have to go to the Devil seven times before they sprout!

The flavour and texture of both types of parsley are crisp and fresh and clean, with a peppery aftertaste that makes you feel somehow more awake. I was never much of a fan of the stuff until I started to cook, when

I found that parsley accentuated so many other dishes, not just as pesto, but in all kinds of soups and stews, sauces and stocks. It is nutritious, too, containing vitamins C, A and K as well as calcium, iron and magnesium. Celery is also a good source of vitamins C, A and K, and contains folate, potassium and antioxidants, too.

Parsley is rarely used as a medicine these days, but was once, like celery, used in various remedies, such as for the healthy functioning of the brain, bladder and kidneys, and in the relief of gout, rheumatism, cramps and even asthma.

Celery and/or Parsley Salad

This is a recipe from John Evelyn (1620–1706), a government official who was also a renowned writer and gardener. It's not clear if he's referring to celery or parsley, but either or both can be used. I have altered the wording slightly to make it more readable.

"The tender leaves of the Blanched Stalk do well in our salad, as likewise the slices of the whitened stems, which being crisp and short, first peeled and slit longwise, are eaten with oil, vinegar, salt and pepper; for its grateful taste is placed in the middle of the Grand Salad, at our Great Men's Tables . . . as the Grace of the whole board."

There is just one disclaimer; he mentions that "Caution is to be given of a small red worm, often lurking in the stalks".

I have never seen this little red worm myself, but if you do, I'd be interested to hear about it.

3. Sage

(Salvia officinalis)

I'm not sure if I can put into words how much I love this herb. As with all these healing garden plants, no matter how pretty they are, it's the scent that carries me to a place that's beyond words; one single breath is enough for the shoulders to drop and all to be right in the world.

There are zillions of different sorts of salvias, some deliberately hybridized, others natural. All of them are, I believe, scented.

HOW TO IDENTIFY SAGE

Common sage (*Salvia officinalis*) can be identified by its aromatic scent and grey-green, veined leaves, which have a furry underside that appears white. Blue or purple flowers appear on spikes and the plant grows up to 75cm (30in) high. Originally native to the Mediterranean region, it likes sunny, dry spots in the garden.

ALL ABOUT SAGE

Sage is believed to help with cognitive function. Just one cup of sage tea in the morning might help, and the aroma is almost otherworldly.

Before we dive further into this wonderful herb, let's find out how the sense of scent works. When we smell something – whether "good" or "bad" – our nose and brain work together to make sense of hundreds of invisible particles (aka molecules or chemicals) floating in the air. If we sniff deliberately, the molecules reach the roof of our nostrils, so we can smell the scent (unless we have a cold). Because we have two nostrils, this means our brain can detect tiny differences in each one. If you block one of your nostrils, you'll sense a difference. *Try it right now.* Even more incredible is that inside our nostrils there are neurons that send electrical messages to the olfactory bulb at the front of the brain, which then sends the info to other areas of the brain. These signals can "turn on" emotions and memories attached to smells, which may be good, bad, frightening, nostalgic or more. Using your sense of smell can give you an unexpected jolt, as latent memories come to the surface.

I don't know for certain why the scent of sage makes me so happy, but I suspect it's the herb itself. Sage is associated with cleanliness, not only because of the refreshing scent, but also due to its use in sage sticks, which are burned to clear negative energy. If there was any doubt as to the efficacy of this plant, look at the botanical name, which clearly tells us what we need to know: *salvia* means "to heal".

One of the most interesting members of this plant family is *Salvia divinorum*, also known as seer's sage or magic mint. *Divinorum* means "Salvia of the ghosts", but the real name according to the botanist who first collected the plant is *Salvia divinatorum* or "Salvia of the priests". In any case, this particular sage has since been outlawed, and may not be bought or sold, because of its strong psychoactive effects. Some plants are best left to the shaman.

Sage Butter Jackets

So simple it's almost laughable, but this will only work if you LOVE sage!

Bake yourself a lovely big jacket potato and, when ready, use a pestle and mortar to grind the herb along with a generous dollop of softened butter. Use as much sage as you like, but a good handful at least.

4. Rosemary

(Salvia rosmarinus)

Another type of sage, rosemary is a stalwart garden herb and valued culinary herb, though not seen so much in private gardens as in former years. I've noticed it used lots in municipal areas, including in big cities where, I imagine, the people hurrying to desk jobs might sweep the narrow leaves with one hand, not even thinking, to release the scent – a small moment of joy. The name of this aromatic plant comes from *ros* (dew) and *marinus* (sea), hence "rose of the sea".

HOW TO IDENTIFY ROSEMARY

Evergreen rosemary has strongly scented needle-like leaves with pale felty undersides and pretty little flowers that can be blue, white or pink. Bushes grow up to 2m (6½ft). Another plant that originated in the Mediterranean, it is nonetheless quite hardy and, once it's mature, will happily stay outside all year round in the UK.

ALL ABOUT ROSEMARY

Although we tend to think of rosemary as something to do with the dead and remembrance, the plant is used in the same way as sage in culinary contexts (such as in a roast dinner) and in cleansing rituals; in herbal medicine rosemary stimulates blood flow, including to the head to improve memory and focus, and is considered a restorative in general. In the olden days, a wedding bouquet would include a sprig of rosemary as a memento of the bride's old home, later pressed into the ground of the new home to say hello to a new life, for both plant and bride.

Rosemary is dedicated to the goddess of love, Aphrodite. There was, at one time, an idea that the health of the woman of the house coincided with the health of the rosemary. I wonder if the emphasis might be that herbs in general belonged to the female? Having said that, the flowers of rosemary are hermaphrodite, having both male and female organs, and the plant has sometimes been considered a masculine one. Roman priests, apparently, used it as an incense, and Christian folklore tells us that the shrub will last for 33 years, the age of Christ at his death, and attain a height of 1.8m (6ft), so that it would never be taller than Christ. The rosemary that came with my house, the previous people told me, was

40 years old, and that was 10 years ago. Although it's now quite gnarly and several bits of it have fallen off, it's got plenty of life left in it. Perhaps I just got lucky, or, most likely, the plant is very special.

Rosemary Tincture

As a tincture, rosemary has many uses. For example, it's a tonic for the nervous system, supports brain function, helps alleviate depression, relieves headaches and is antimicrobial; you get the picture.

1. First, harvest some rosemary flowers and leaves. If a couple of the stems want to play too, let them.

2. Place in a clean, sterilized jar, approx. 250ml/9fl oz/1 cup, and cover with 80 per cent proof vodka or gin.

3. Let the jar sit, out of the sun, for at least 8 weeks. Shake on a regular basis.

4. When the tincture is ready, strain the liquid, using a tea strainer and fine muslin, letting it drip into a dropper bottle. Don't strain the liquid any further as it may go cloudy. Store in a cool, dry place and it will last for years.

The same process can be used for different herbs, so you will soon have a lovely set of tinctures for all needs.

5. Thyme

(Thymus vulgaris)

Next up is thyme, another modest but mighty herb. Originating in the Mediterranean basin and a member of the mint family, *Thymus vulgaris* is the most popular plant in the species. The name *thymus*, meaning "to fumigate", is a reminder that the plant was burned as incense.

HOW TO IDENTIFY THYME

Thyme is small, up to 30cm (12in), generally with a woody stem that becomes gnarly when older. In early spring, tiny pink, lilac or lavender blossoms are nearly invisible under the mass of bees. Thyme doesn't bother about rich soil or poor, so long as the ground isn't waterlogged. If you don't have access to a garden but would still like some, thyme is also easily found in packets in supermarkets or in pots to keep on a windowsill.

ALL ABOUT THYME

In ancient Greece and Rome, thyme was an important symbol of power, strength, courage and sacrifice, its image embroidered onto the togas of the most important generals. During the Crusades, thyme was given to the knights about to go into battle, with the idea of giving them strength.

There are many health benefits of thyme, too. Nicholas Culpeper called it a "notable strengthener of the lungs" and said it was a remedy for whooping cough. People still use it for respiratory issues (see opposite) and hay fever, as well as to treat bites, stings, fungal infections and intestinal worms!

At the time of writing, it's 18 October, St Luke's Day. Lucky for me, there are marigolds (*Calendula officinalis*) in the garden, needed for a charm in his honour. I take sprigs of marigold and thyme and dry them in front of a fire until they crumble. I sift them through fine linen, put them in a saucepan with honey and vinegar and simmer over a low flame. I then rub the mixture on myself and repeat the following three times:

"St Luke, St Luke,
be kind to me
In dreams let
my true love see."

All I have to do is sleep, hoping to see a vision of my true love. There's one ingredient missing – wormwood (*Artemisia absinthium*) – but it's worth the effort anyway.

I love these strange rituals and charms that remind us of childhood. Sometimes I can hear the kids next door inventing their own magical games. No one is telling them what to do or how to do it. Like us, they are looking for magic in whatever form that might take.

Thyme Cough Remedy

The microbial properties of thyme have been used for many years in treating lung infections, such as an annoying chesty cough. My favourite thyme remedy is a simple hot tea, with honey and lemon and a few thyme stems and leaves, steeped and drunk as needed.

All you need to do is to add 1 tablespoon of fresh thyme (or 1 teaspoon of the dried herb) to a teapot or mug, add boiling water, then cover and leave for 10 minutes to steep. Strain the thyme, add honey to taste and (if you like) a slice of lemon, and sip thankfully.

6. Lemon Balm

(Melissa officinalis)

This is the only plant in this chapter that you can't buy in the supermarket, though you can get a pot of it in the garden centre. Lemon balm is a distinctly renegade little being, one foot still in the gutter despite its beauty, fragrance and usefulness. If ever there was a plant that was ripped up, burned or binned, it's lemon balm, seen by many gardeners as invasive. But the name, *melissa* ("bee"), tells us that bees love this plant, and this fact alone is enough to make any nature lover decide to love it too. If in any further doubt, the word balm – which means blessing – tells you that this plant is a friend for us.

HOW TO IDENTIFY LEMON BALM

Lemon balm has oval, wrinkled leaves and the square stems seen in other members of Lamiaceae (the mint family). With this herb, most people "get it" not by looks, but by its fresh, citrusy smell. I don't often see lemon balm on foraging trips unless I'm in a wasteland area, such as an abandoned building or other places where humans used to live. Sometimes, when we are in unfamiliar places, it is hard to work out what we are looking at, even if it's something common. Lemon balm is easy to grow in a garden; it has a tendency to take over the flowerbed.

ALL ABOUT LEMON BALM

Pop lemon balm's leaves in your pocket to sniff at if you are anxious or nervous, such as when doing exams (which often take place in the heat of summer, the perfect time to be able to find the plant and use it to keep clear, calm and collected).

Once upon a time, it is said, beekeepers used to rub lemon balm leaves inside the older hives, encouraging the young bees to take over the desirable residence. Also, in Italy, if you were a woman who happened to find lemon balm, the tradition was to crush the leaf pending the day of your death, with a prayer that Christ would assist you to heaven.

Lemon balm makes for a cooling summer drink: take some leaves, muddle them (that is, crush them until almost liquid), add honey and mint and then strain. This makes a refreshing drink that is soothing if you are feeling hot and bothered after a day in the sun.

Carmelite Water

The original recipe for Carmelite water, the herbal spirit made by the Carmelite Nuns of St Just, has changed through the ages. It has been marketed as Eau de Carmes and Eau de Mélisse, and it's likely there were other recipes. For those with an excess of lemon balm, this refreshing, citrusy herbal tonic – part medicine and part pleasure – is a game changer. Once you get the idea, play about with the ingredients to make your own version. Alcohol is generally an ingredient, but you can bypass that by freezing it.

You will need:
4 tbsp dried lemon balm leaves
3 tbsp dried angelica leaves
2 tbsp whole cloves (can be reused)
1 tbsp whole coriander seeds
1–2 tsp sugar or alternative, to taste
1 cinnamon stick
455ml/16fl oz/2 cups vodka (or water)

1. Place the aromatics and sugar in a sterilized glass jar and add vodka (or water). Keep the ingredients under the liquid. If the jar's lid is metal, use baking parchment to separate the metal from the liquid.

2. Label and date the jar. Shake daily for 3–4 weeks.

3. Strain the liquid into a clean, sterilized bottle and keep in a cool dark place. If using water rather than spirits, the shelf-life will not be quite as good unless you freeze it. Keep in a cool place for two weeks, then freeze.

4. Serve with ice and mint in the summer months.

If you have so much lemon balm that you can't think of anything else to do with it, bundle up the stems and leaves, tie with cotton and allow them to dry out to make firelighters.

7. Tarragon

(Artemisia dracunculus)

Aha! Here's a cousin of our beloved mugwort. Tarragon, also known as dragon sagewort, is *Artemisia dracunculus*. And *dracunculus*, in Latin, means "little dragon". All very Harry Potter! It is the twisting roots of this herb which give the name.

HOW TO IDENTIFY TARRAGON

Tarragon has long, narrow, scented leaves and small yellow flowers. It grows wild in Eurasia and North America, but not in the UK. In common with other mugworts, tarragon is aromatic. If you're ever in a situation in which you need to identify which is Russian tarragon and which is French tarragon (happens all the time), then you need to know that the Russian kind smells like sweet grass, but the French kind is more like aniseed. Also, Russian tarragon doesn't need much looking after – I leave mine in a smallish pot over winter, and so far it has always come back. But French tarragon can only be propagated by cuttings.

ALL ABOUT TARRAGON

Tarragon (and the whole sprawling family) is named after Artemis, moon goddess for the ancient Greeks and known as Diana to the Romans. The herb is also favoured by Lilith, Adam's first wife, who quit Eden when she realized that Adam wanted her to be subservient. She has had a bad reputation ever since, said to be a child-murderer and seducer of men.

In the Middle Ages, tarragon was used as a remedy for breathlessness, with asthmatic conditions no doubt brought on by living in damp, smoky houses. The Greeks used the herb to numb the pain of toothache. Tarragon is said to help with digestive issues, too, including an upset stomach. It is also reputed to help you sleep. If you have enough of the stuff, dry the leaves to use inside a herbal sleep pillow.

Tarragon Dressing

This is very simple indeed, with only three ingredients: tarragon, olive oil and parsley.

All you need to do is blend the ingredients together; for a more authentic medieval feel when doing this, use a pestle and mortar.

Use as a dressing for cold or warm salads, and if there is anything left over, mop it up with some slightly stale bread and eat when no one is watching.

8. Basil

(Ocimum basilicum)

This plant has many names and many different kinds: sweet basil, common basil, royal basil, and more. And although we might suppose that basil originates in the Mediterranean, its home could equally be in India or Iran. We are lucky to have this herb relatively easy to hand pretty much wherever we are on the planet.

HOW TO IDENTIFY BASIL

Basil can't survive frost, but the seeds are easy to grow indoors. This is another member of Lamiaceae, the mint family, so has the characteristic square stems plus shiny, somewhat cupped oval leaves with a pointed tip. The smell, of course, is the big giveaway.

ALL ABOUT BASIL

In Italian and Greek folklore, basil has meanings that are polar opposites: it is an erotic symbol, but also a symbol of mourning. In earlier days, young girls wore the plant as a symbol of virginity, whereas married women also wore basil in their hair, to show their marital status.

Basil was also believed to be a sexual stimulant, for horses as well as people. In Tuscany, basil is called *amorino*, and if a man wanted a girl to fall in love with him, all he had to do was place the herb on her windowsill. However, there is a darker side to this plant. On the island of Crete, it was considered the plant of the Devil, this time placed on the windowsill as a warning of his coming. One wonders how often these habits might have got mixed up. And in the days of Elizabeth I of England, it was believed that a woman in labour would feel no pain at all if she held a basil root and the feather of a swallow. Would this work?

Some people believed that scorpions can be born from finely ground basil left under a stone, and that worms crawl out of basil left out in the sun. A similar notion held that basil, if beaten in river water, would attract scorpions.

Some Hindu marriages are celebrated between trees. One of these bridal trees is holy basil (*Ocimum tenuiflorum*), a sacred herb of the reincarnation of Krishna. It is said that good Hindus meet their end clutching a basil leaf, as a sort of passport to Paradise. Be aware that eating holy basil, unlike the other kinds of basil, can cause nausea or diarrhoea.

Among other uses, basil is a cough suppressant and sedative as well as a general stimulant and a tonic. Basil can also be used as a tea, refreshing and invigorating. It is said that basil enhances mental health, the digestive system, and also regulates blood sugar levels.

Basil is delicious as a culinary herb and can be used in as many ways as you have imagination; try basil and pecorino pesto swirled into a cold soup on a hot day.

If you have a headache, simply pour hot water over a bowl of basil leaves, hang your head over the bowl, and cover your head with a towel in the time-worn way. All you need to do is inhale the healing, aromatic steam for as long as you need.

9. Lavender

(Lavandula angustifolia)

The last garden herb in our sights is one that many people adore. This plant originated, as so many do, in the Mediterranean basin. These days, it is a tame garden plant, cultivated by gardeners of all ages for that wonderful scent. The name is believed to come from the Latin *lavare*, meaning "to wash".

HOW TO IDENTIFY LAVENDER

Lavender grows in bushes with long, narrow leaves and the distinctive beautifully scented purple or blue flower spikes. As you might imagine for a plant that once upon a time thrived in hot conditions, lavender prefers a sunny spot; right now, as I am typing, I am looking at snowy ground and wondering if my own lavenders will come through the winter unscathed. I have a feeling that they just might.

ALL ABOUT LAVENDER

Hildegard of Bingen (a German Benedictine Abbess, composer, mystic, philosopher and, laterly, a saint) said that lavender, along with other herbs, could ward off evil spirits, and, given the scent, who could think otherwise?

Clean, crisp and cooling, it is the essential oil made from the stalks and flowers of lavender that we value for its calming and relaxing properties. It was supposed that the Romans were the first to use the plant for its scent, perfuming their bathwater and scattering dried heads to repel moths, but who knows? People still use lavender bags as a natural moth repellent.

There are some strange and unlikely folkloric ideas about this herb. Did you know that lavender is said to have got its clean scent when Jesus was a baby and Mary hung his clean clothes on a bush to dry?

In olden times, newlywed girls would put lavender under the pillow to avoid arguments, as well as ensure marital passion. These days, lavender is more likely to be used to help promote sleep.

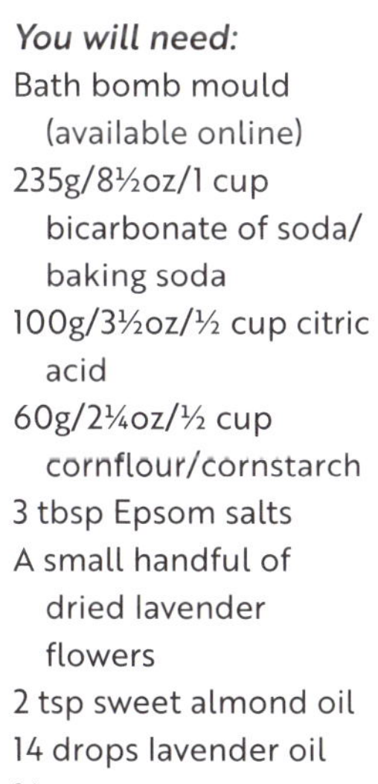

Lavender Bath Bombs

These are really lovely – if you like lavender, that is. You can also use rose petals, calendula or a mix of herbs.

You will need:
Bath bomb mould (available online)
235g/8½oz/1 cup bicarbonate of soda/baking soda
100g/3½oz/½ cup citric acid
60g/2¼oz/½ cup cornflour/cornstarch
3 tbsp Epsom salts
A small handful of dried lavender flowers
2 tsp sweet almond oil
14 drops lavender oil
¾ tsp water

1. In a large bowl, mix the bicarbonate of soda/baking soda, citric acid, cornflour/cornstarch, Epsom salts and dried lavender.

2. In a small bowl, combine the almond oil, lavender oil and water.

3. Pour the wet mixture into the dry mixture and whisk until combined.

4. Test by pressing a handful of the mixture. If it doesn't hold lightly together, spray with water using a spray bottle a couple of times until it begins to clump.

5. Press the mixture into your mould and let dry for at least 3 hours to harden before use.

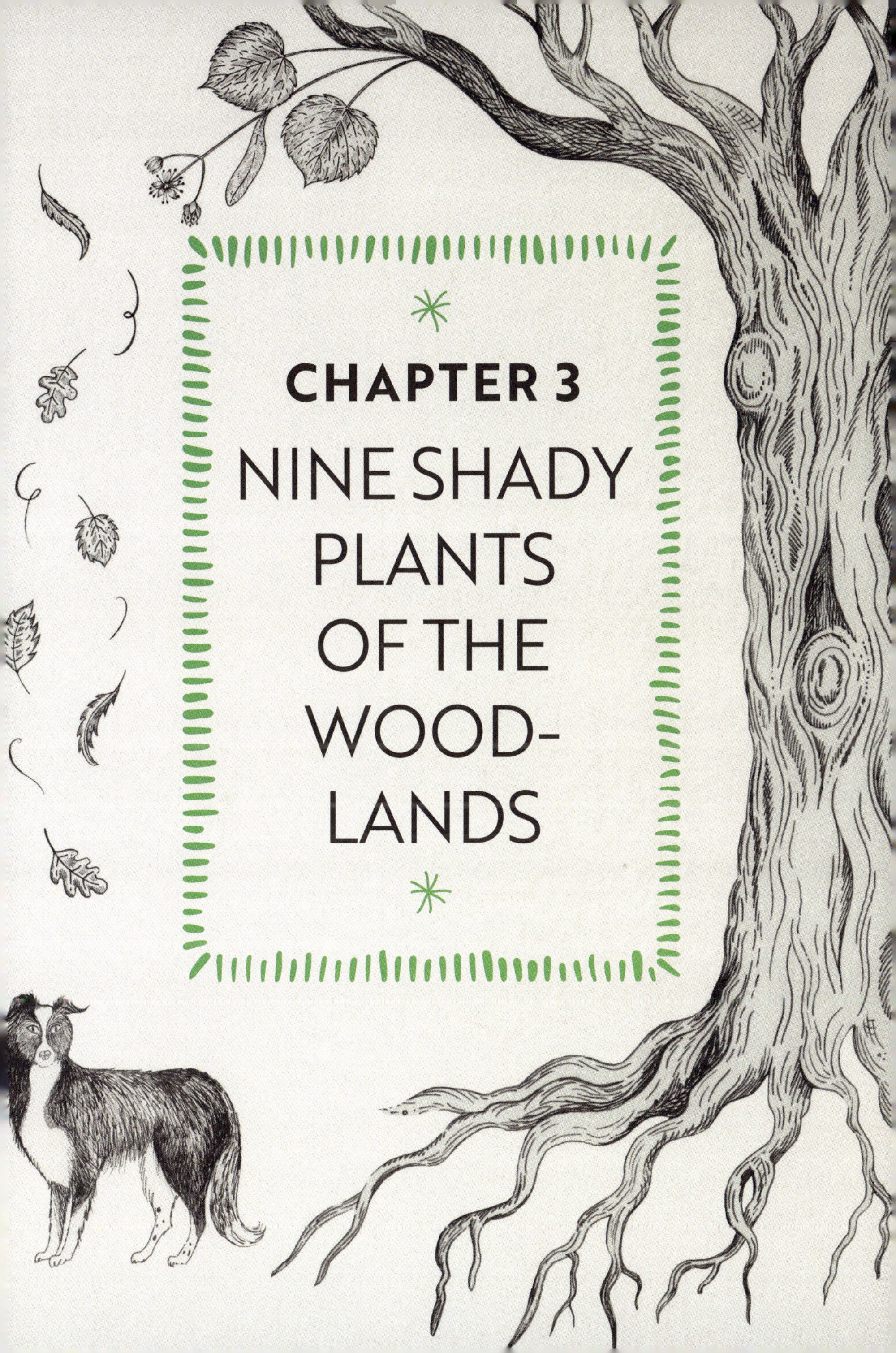

CHAPTER 3

NINE SHADY PLANTS OF THE WOOD-LANDS

Nine Shady Plants of the Woodlands

Trees are our guardians, providing so much when we give them so little. Some of their generosity is easy to recognize: food, medicine, shelter and shade, for example, as well as essentials that we might not immediately think of, such as oxygen, carbon storage, pollutant removal and noise reduction. There's also their contribution to our sense of health and wellbeing. So let's now meander through the forests of our imagination, and find out about the nine shady herbs of the woodlands. Technically speaking, trees are not herbs, but we can bend a few rules here and there in the cause of foraging and the sheer breathtaking loveliness of these beings.

Here's a thought I had recently about a tree. It was a rainy day, early November, and I was trudging up the usual hill that's ideal for a quick half-hour dog walk. The trees were whippy, leaves tugging from the branches and clattering to the ground as though they couldn't wait to get away. As I pushed along, head down, I wondered what the trees might think of me. I stopped to imagine what the tree could see. What I saw was this.

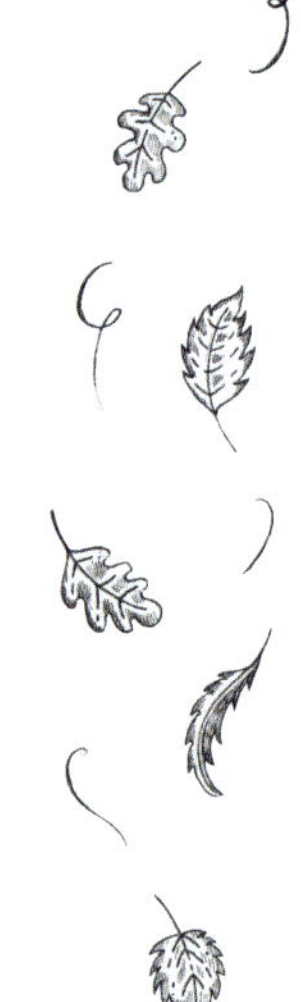

The tree could see me, alone, attached only with a rope to a smaller creature (my dog). The dog was also, to all intents and purposes, alone. The tree was sorry for me and the dog. "All alone", I imagined the tree was saying. "These are lonely creatures, not connected, having to do everything themselves. Where is the community?"

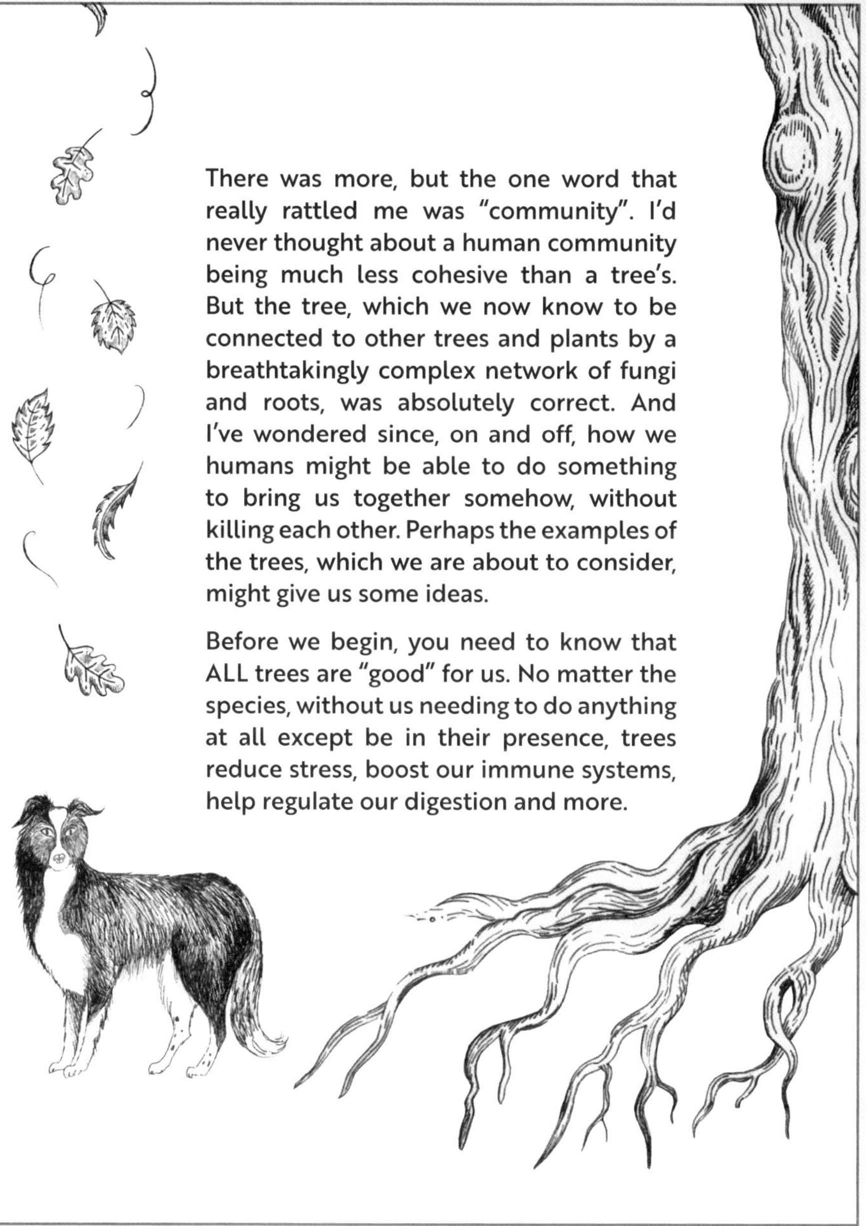

There was more, but the one word that really rattled me was "community". I'd never thought about a human community being much less cohesive than a tree's. But the tree, which we now know to be connected to other trees and plants by a breathtakingly complex network of fungi and roots, was absolutely correct. And I've wondered since, on and off, how we humans might be able to do something to bring us together somehow, without killing each other. Perhaps the examples of the trees, which we are about to consider, might give us some ideas.

Before we begin, you need to know that ALL trees are "good" for us. No matter the species, without us needing to do anything at all except be in their presence, trees reduce stress, boost our immune systems, help regulate our digestion and more.

1. Alder

(Alnus glutinosa)

Alder encompasses various species, mostly native to the northern hemisphere. For the alder to work its magic, it needs to sit in water. Most wood breaks down in waterlogged conditions, but the alder has a sort of superpower, able to withstand wet conditions for thousands of years, in time becoming petrified, just like stone!

HOW TO IDENTIFY ALDER

This is a deciduous tree, with dark brown bark often covered in lichens. Leaves are alternate, a rounded shape, and the purple buds that emerge in the late winter/early spring are sticky to the touch. The flowers appear before the leaves, arranged as cone-like catkins, easy to see in the winter when there are scant leaves. Both male and female catkins are found on the same tree. Male catkins dangle, measuring 2–6cm (¾–2½in), and turn yellow, while female catkins are oval, green and are grouped in clusters of three to eight on each stalk (these get woodier with age and can be made into tiny models of bees). Alder trees love to grow in wet conditions such as marshes and streams.

ALL ABOUT ALDER

Alder roots help to prevent soil erosion. If you have ever been to Venice, you might have noticed wooden piles emerging from the depths; there are millions of them driven into the seabed and without them the city would not exist. Some of these alder piles, it is said, were there at the very beginning of the city.

> *"Alder for shoes*
> *Do wise men choose"*

This little ditty refers to the traditional use of alder wood for making clogs. This still happens, although handmade clogs are a big ticket these days, fetching from £200 or more. There's even a clogmaker not so far from where I live, on the Welsh borders. I spent a wonderful time chatting with him in his atmospheric shop, among the wood shavings, lasts, leather, delicious old-smelling wood and the sparky tang of metal. The clogmaker told me that he had almost given up the business as there was diminishing demand for such a specialist product. Then he was featured in a glossy magazine, then a similar TV show, and now he is so busy that he is considering taking on an apprentice. He also told me that so much alder had been used to make clogs that, in some areas of Wales, it was called *pren clocsia*, or "clog wood" in Welsh.

Fever, toothache and even warts were thought, at one time, to be able to transfer, magically, to an alder. Alder leaves can be used as a gargle for sore throats.

2. Willow

(Salix alba)

There are many different species of willow with a huge number of folk names, such as gorgy-mill tree, willy tree, withy, duck willow, pussy willow and many more. One of the species is called the English Cricket Bat Willow (*Salix Alba Caerulea*). This variety grows all over the world and hybridizes naturally. It is a merger of white willow (*Salix alba*) and crack willow (*Salix fragilis*). I'm describing here the very popular white willow, which is a beautiful sight sweeping its branches across a river, silvery leaves dancing in the breeze.

HOW TO IDENTIFY WILLOW

A mature *Salix alba* can grow up to 30m (100ft), with brown/grey bark that becomes fissured with age, and slender, flexible twigs of the same colour. The oval leaves help with identification, as they have a covering of silky, silvery hairs on the underside. The catkins appear in the early springtime, with male and female flowers growing on separate trees. The female catkins are slightly shorter than the male ones, but after pollination they become longer and develop capsules, each one containing miniature seeds covered in fluffy white down that helps wind dispersal.

ALL ABOUT WEEPING WILLOW

Myths and legends of willow are abundant. The "weeping" kind was dedicated to Juno/Hera, goddess of women and guardian of marriage; effigies of her were carved from its wood. The willow was also the tree of Persephone, goddess of the underworld. Her lover, Orpheus, is sometimes depicted holding a willow branch in his hand. Then there's Jason (of the Argonauts fame) who found a field of alarming willows from which bodies wrapped in cowskins were suspended, waiting for the men to be reincarnated.

The symbolism of plants is often linked to their looks or habits, and willow is no exception. That the willow "weeps" is down to its habit of trailing leaves and branches, and depictions of the tree in art symbolize grief. In Victorian times, the term "she wears the willow" meant that the grieving woman had sworn that she would never remarry.

Willow has a reputation for being evil, perhaps because of the gloomy, watery conditions that the tree loves. However, it is one of the most common and useful medicinal plants, and has been so for many years. Hippocrates (*c.*460–*c.*370 BCE) prescribed the use of willow bark against the pain of rheumatism; the key ingredient, salicylic acid, is still used today for a range of remedies including pain relief. You can make a simple decoction of willow: boil some bark shavings in water, strain, leave to cool and sip for the relief of pain, inflammation or fever.

3. Black Poplar

(Populus nigra)

Black poplar, native to northwest Europe, western Asia, northern Africa and regions of the USA, seems to be something of a loner, with other more gregarious trees looking on, possibly wondering who the shy guy is. There are only 7,000 black poplars left in the UK, of which fewer than 600 are female trees. Its scarcity means that the few remaining trees are unlikely to pollinate one another. Other trees do pollinate black poplar, but this just produces hybrids, making matters worse. This is the most threatened tree species in the whole of Europe.

HOW TO IDENTIFY BLACK POPLAR

Black poplars like to have their feet in a ditch. The profile of the tree is distinctive, quite lopsided with huge branches both low down and high up, as though the tree was just waiting for itself to fall. A mature black poplar tree will grow to some 30m (100ft), with a lifespan of 200 years. Bark is dark brown but can seem to be black, with thick gnarly fissures. Young leaves are an elegant heart shape, with long tips. Rub the leaves together for a cool balsam scent. Male and female flowers can be found on separate trees; the bright red male catkins are a good way to identify the tree even when the leaves are not there. The fertilized female catkins morph into fluffy cottony seeds, which will fall later in the summer.

ALL ABOUT BLACK POPLAR (AND A MENTION OF THE WHITE ONE, TOO)

The black tree is dedicated to Hades, god of the underworld and death, but the white poplar belongs to his wife, Persephone, goddess of resurrection.

Although the use of black poplar would now be frowned upon because of the tree's scarcity, it's still interesting to know how it was used as medicine. Powder made from the bark of the young branches, mixed with oak and white willow, was used to alleviate fevers. In Flanders, sprouting black poplar buds were cooked in lard (with no salt) and cow's butter in the month of May to make a good all-round ointment, used against fevers and insomnia.

In latter-day herbal remedies, the leaf buds, bark of two-year-old branches and wood shavings are combined in a remedy to reduce phlegm, stimulate digestion, heal wounds and encourage sweat. This medicine is still in use by specialists who know the tree and can use it properly without damaging it.

If you find a black poplar, take a cutting and plant it in a place that you now know the plant will like. Thank you!

4. English Elm & 5. Wych Elm

(Ulmus procera & Ulmus glabra)

The English elm (*Ulmus procera*), which is also found in the USA, was once a common sight, on par with the oak as a symbol of England. However, this all changed due to the work of a tiny insect, the elm bark beetle, which was introduced to the UK from Canada in the late 1960s and spread the fungal Dutch elm disease. So far over *60 million* trees have died in the UK, mainland Europe and North America.

However, while the outlook for English elm remains bleak, it's not all bad news for elms. This is where another elm species strides into the forest – the wych elm (*Ulmus glabra*). "Wych" means flexible. Although attacked by Dutch elm disease too, this elm is much hardier.

HOW TO IDENTIFY ENGLISH ELM AND WYCH ELM

English elm and wych elm are often confused. The trees grow to a similar height (30m/100ft), bear red-purple fruits that turn into the distinctive winged seeds called "samara", and their leaves are oval with toothed edges and the asymmetric base that is characteristic of elm leaves (leaving a bit of stalk bare on one side). However, English elm leaves are smaller and more rounded, and the asymmetry is less noticeable. In practice, you're so much less likely to find an English elm due to the prevalence of the disease. Look for wych elms in rocky places or near streams and ditches.

ALL ABOUT ELM

The elm was such an important tree, for many generations, that it's hard to imagine the grief as people realized that the tree was dying. This was often the tree that was planted deliberately in places such as the village square, where people could meet, gathering in the evenings to talk about the events of the day, maybe a song and a dance and off to the hostelry.

In the Mediterranean region, grape vines were for centuries grown between the branches of the elm with the idea that the best grapes came from the highest branches. Historically, elm was used to make a range of items, from clogs and furniture to rifle butts and coffins. Like the alder, its wood is resistant to water, so it was also used for ships and water pipes as well as wine presses.

Not so very long ago, the elm was believed to ward off evil spirits and witches. If you had a staff of the wood, then you could beat up the actual Devil! In England, a twig of elm would break any spells that had curdled the buttermilk. In Germany, just before World War II, elms were still being used as "rag and nail trees". The idea was that fevers and other ailments could be transferred to the trees by hammering the rags into them. In Bedfordshire, Beaumont's Tree was an elm said to have grown from a stake stuck through the body of a murderer. People used to nail toenail clippings and hair to the tree, as a cure for various ailments. Would that work? Who knows?

In herbal medicine, the tannin-rich inner bark of the elm is still used for its fortifying, blood-purifying, astringent properties. Extracts of the bark and leaves are used as a gargle or mouthwash.

Wych elm seeds, or samara, have a lovely sweet flavour and are a good protein-rich snack when you're out foraging. Pleasantly aromatic, they also make a good breath freshener.

6. Larch

(Larix decidua)

Here, we are looking at the European larch (*Larix decidua*), which, although indigenous to central Europe, is widely used in other parts of the world, including the USA. It was introduced into the UK in the early 17th century for timber plantations (the trunks grow tall and strong) and the European settlers in America found it useful for the same reason.

HOW TO IDENTIFY LARCH

This is a tall tree, some 35m (115ft) high. The tree is easy to identify (depending on the time of year) because, unlike other conifers, the leaves twirl down in the autumn, just like any other deciduous tree. Those soft "leaves" are like needles, some 2–4cm (¾–1½in) long, growing in cute knobby tufts on the twigs, before they turn to gold. The shoot tips of the female are little flowers, sometimes called "larch roses", which grow in clusters of green, white or pink. The colours of larch are mesmerizing, especially in the early spring, when they form a delicate rainbow, best seen on a sparkling rainy day (as good a reason to get a dog as any I can think of).

ALL ABOUT LARCH

Once upon a time, larch was revered during pilgrimages, especially in mountainous areas of central Europe. Wooden effigies were carved in honour of the Holy Virgin, possibly as a thanks for a difficult journey that ended safely. As a sacred tree, its wood was not to be gathered in the immediate vicinity, and absolute silence had to be kept by visitors and pilgrims alike.

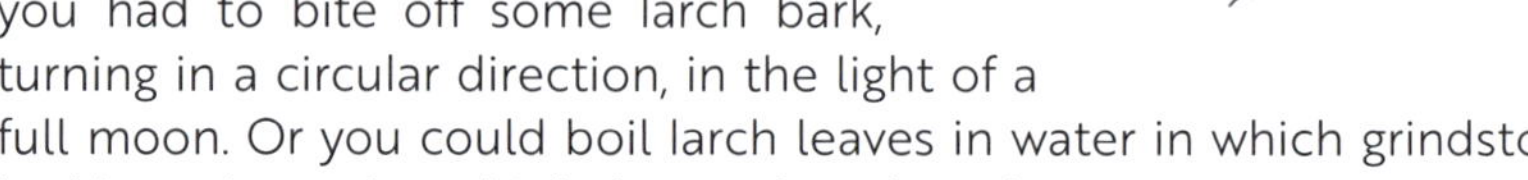

If you had an agonizing toothache, the extracted tooth should be hammered into a larch so that the other teeth would never play the same trick again. If you had a goitre (swelling of the neck), then you had to bite off some larch bark, turning in a circular direction, in the light of a full moon. Or you could boil larch leaves in water in which grindstones had been kept, then drink the resulting liquid.

The sticky gum that can be seen oozing from the bark is said to support gut health. The gum is used to make poultices to help heal coughs and colds and sore throats, too. Also, steam from the bark is used as an expectorant. The Indigenous Peoples of North America used the gum extracted from under the bark as a dressing for cuts and bruises. The leaves and stems of larch have been found to be antiseptic, appetite stimulating and blood purifying.

The largest known larch was witnessed in log form by Pliny the Elder in 77 CE. He said it was 37m (120ft) high, with a thickness of 0.6m (2ft). The Roman Emperor Tiberius had it installed on the deck of an ocean-going ship, a status symbol to end them all!

Larch Picture Frame

In spring, gather larch roses – enough to cover a picture frame. Use a glue gun to attach the larch roses to the frame. Leave until set, then admire your handiwork.

7. Lime

(Tilia spp.*)*

There are at least 30 species of this tree, including the common lime *(Tilia* x *europaea)*, Caucasian lime *(Tilia* x *euchlora)*, a silver lime/linden *(Tilia tomentosa)* and an American lime *(Tilia americana)*. They readily cross-breed, meaning that there are numerous hybrids. "Lime" here has nothing to do with the citrus fruit of the same name. It has several different folk names: linden, spoonwood (guess why), whitewood, basswood and more.

Here's a story about a lime tree. We were a small foraging group: a couple, a family of four, a few more, and an older lady, on her own and joining in happily. We found a beautiful lime tree, not yet blossoming. The woman told me there was a song about the tree; I usually have music in my pocket, so I told her the name of the song: "Linden Lea" by Ralph Vaughan Williams. The woman's eyes widened; then she asked if she could take over the forage for a little while. Of course she could!

She asked us to sit under the canopy of the tree. We did so, and she gulped a couple of times, going a little red; but then she started to sing, soon eclipsing the music coming from the phone as her voice gained confidence. A couple of passers by stopped to listen. It was as though we were in a church. Her voice was astonishing. We were spellbound!

Her story? She had been a mezzo-soprano, quite well known, travelling the world in her singing career. But her son died, aged 22. She stopped singing for years . . . until that day.

This is the sort of thing that can happen when you think you're going foraging, and this is what healing can be.

HOW TO IDENTIFY LIME

Lime trees usually grow to 4.5–6m (15–20ft), though you can get dwarf varieties, too. Leaves are heart-shaped and coarsely toothed; underneath the ribbed "corners" of those leaves, you might see little tufts, home to leaf mites. In summer, the yellow petals give off a heartbreakingly lovely scent; if you wanted to name the scent as an ice cream, I would suggest that it might be named "Honey Vanilla Jasmine".

As the tree ages, the brown-grey trunks become deeply fissured. This tree lends itself to "pleaching", a way of training trees to make a screen or even a tunnel; the process is time consuming (sometimes taking generations) and is most often seen in stately homes.

ALL ABOUT LIME

Tilia has been known to be sacred for thousands of years, and continues to be so for many of us who love this tree. Freya, Norse goddess of love and fertility, is connected with the lime, which is also the tree of love. Therefore, if a couple wanted to marry, all they needed to do was give a vow of undying love underneath the tree. It was only in 1930 that the last couple married, in Germany, under the entwined boughs of the tree.

Lime also could administer justice. Judges used to sit under the tree to help them "to do the right thing", the tree acting as an external conscience. I like both these ideas – wouldn't it be great if we could uphold these traditions?

Witches, fairies and nymphs are said to hide in the fissures of the bark of many trees, the lime included. Some of these witch trees were known by name; one of them was called "Tileal", but I hesitate to say the name out loud. If you come upon a particularly magical looking lime, have a chat and see what happens. We are only a wish away from a different way of feeling and thinking. The Baltic goddess of fate and luck, Laima, is associated with the lime tree. She appears as a cuckoo to hand out her prognostications.

If you have ever noticed the decorative filigree wood carvings in English churches and stately homes, you might be surprised to find that lime is likely to be the material used. The soft inner bark, or "bast", allows the carving of these intricate patterns.

Lime leaves, boiled or used fresh and crushed, were used as a poultice to help to heal a wound. As described below, lime blossom tea is a wonderful all-round remedy!

Lime Blossom Tea

Lime blossom tea is good for coughs and colds; you can dry the flowers to use when needed in the autumn and winter. The blossom is stimulating, with diuretic properties. Lime blossom tea also dissolves mucus in the bronchial cavities and, as a cosmetic use, the same water is used not only to calm down freckles, but also to get rid of wrinkles!

Pour boiling water over fresh or dried lime blossoms
and leave to infuse for at least 5 minutes.
Strain, sweeten with honey if liked, and drink.

Forager's Choice by Natasha Lloyd

I met Natasha via the Forager's Association. She works in Scotland and is a forager, a teacher and a medical herbalist with a BSc (Hons) in herbal medicine. She is a Director of the National Institute of Medical Herbalists. You can find her on Instagram as @gathering.nature, and her first book, *Foraged Condiments*, is exquisite.

Natasha's Tilia and Pear Chutney

This is a delicate and light chutney that helps you relax (lime flowers are wonderful for relaxation and have been shown to help reduce plaque build-up in arteries). I think they taste like honeyed pear, so they work well with pears and apples.

You will need:

2 tsp sunflower oil
1 onion, finely chopped
5g/⅛oz fresh or dried lime flowers
2 pears, peeled, cored and cut into pieces
1 tbsp sugar or natural sweetener of your choice
1 tsp sea salt
1 tbsp apple cider vinegar

1. Heat the oil in a small saucepan, then add the onion and cook for a few minutes until translucent but not brown.

2. Add the lime flowers, pear, sugar, salt and vinegar. Allow this to cook until the pears start to break down, adding some water if required so that the mixture doesn't stick to the bottom of the pan. Take if off the heat once the pears have broken down and all the ingredients have started to come together.

3. Allow to cool slightly, then transfer to a clean, sterilized jar. Wait for it to cool completely before closing the lid.

4. This can be eaten straight away but is better if you leave it for a month or two.

8. Rowan

(Sorbus aucuparia)

There's a whole raft of folk names for rowan, which should give us an insight into the tree: checker tree, mountain ash, picken, quickbeam, service tree, Thor's helper, witchwood, and many more. Some people associate the English word rowan with the tree's Old Norse name *runa*, meaning "magic".

HOW TO IDENTIFY ROWAN

The tree is deciduous, with long slim branches and smooth greyish bark. The pinnate leaves look very much like those of a rose, so it is no surprise that the flower is a cousin of the tree. Five-petalled, cream-white flowers develop into abundant clusters of bright red or yellow, round berries. The mountain ash moniker is because of rowan's love of heights and similarity to the shape of the ash tree.

SAFETY: **Cook or freeze rowan berries before consuming to remove the toxic parasorbic acid.**

ALL ABOUT ROWAN

This tree is steeped in magic. For the Druids, the tree acts as a gateway that can transport you into another world. It was dedicated to Thor, god of thunder. The bright red berries were said to heal wounded warriors (although some of the berries are yellow, I find, so I don't know if that would make a difference). Runes, or "fate sticks", were cut from the tree, with permission from the rowan itself.

More than anything, this tree has a protective force and it is believed to repel witches, though it also grows where you would expect witches to live. In Denmark, remnants of rowan twigs have been found in Bronze Age graves along with other items that look as though they might have protective uses. Across Britain, branches of rowan were hung above the stalls of animals; Scottish shepherds made their sheep pass under them. Rowan was also hung in or planted outside homes with the aim of keeping the witches out, and bowls and utensils were made from rowan wood for the same reason.

Pliny the Elder tells us that rowan was used effectively in instances of dysentery and other disorders of the stomach. In latter-day herbal medicine, the dried leaves and boiled berries have a laxative effect, also used to bring about menstruation. Rowan berries are high in vitamin C and were once used as a remedy against scurvy – try making them into a jelly or jam. Or, if you know where to find a decent crop of rowan berries, harvest them when ripe and keep in the refrigerator for the birds, saving them for the worst of the winter.

You could also use a few of them to make a rowan necklace or bracelet. Leave the berries outside the fridge to dry and harden until they are stable, then thread the "beads" to make a rosary. Wear this to carry rowan's protective qualities with you.

9. Oak

(Quercus spp.)

Some 600 species of oak have been in existence much longer than us humans, dating back to about 44 to 56 million years ago (these numbers are speculative), and native to the northern hemisphere, such as China, the Americas and the Himalayas .

Oak in Sanskrit is *deru*, which also means "tree". This is also the root of the words Druid, duir (the Irish word for "oak") and door; the oak therefore not only embodies the essence of a tree but itself is a door, a gateway to inner wisdom for those who seek it.

HOW TO IDENTIFY OAK

Oak can be identified by its acorns and often by a pleasing spreading silhouette that seems to display nature's artistry at its highest. Bark is silvery brown and smooth but becomes fissured and gnarly in older trees. The leaves are lobed; a *Quercus robur* leaf has four or five rounded, smooth-edged lobes, while a *Quercus alba* leaf has seven to nine more pointed lobes. Another way to tell the different types of oak apart is to look at their acorns: *Quercus robur* acorns grow on longer stalks, *Quercus alba* acorns have short stalks, and the acorns of *Quercus petrea*, or sessile oak, have very short or no stalks at all.

ALL ABOUT OAK

Next time you see an oak, remember that it was (is) the tree of the gods, sacred to the thunder gods Zeus, Jupiter and Thor (it was thought to be the tree most frequently struck by lightning), as well as being associated with the Irish god Dagda and, of course, the Druids. Oak wood was burned at festivities, in honour of the gods, and the worship of both god and tree became inextricably mixed. Look with your inner eyes and perhaps you'll see what those ancient people saw.

Many of us still believe what the ancient Greeks and Romans believed; that an old oak was a mythical world in itself. It was a microcosm full of tree nymphs, dryads and hamadryads as well as other creatures, "real" or otherwise; the woodpecker, the bee and the magpie are example of real creatures that have a mythical side too. The Woodland Trust in the UK tells us that 2,300 different species rely on the oak for food, shelter and breeding. No other tree species supports a greater diversity of life, magical or otherwise, than an old oak.

The oak was put to use in ancient Greece in a divinatory practice called "dendromancy", in which the Oak Oracle spoke through Pleiades ("doves"), holy priestesses who interpreted the rustling of the oak trees.

Oak trees can grow to a grand age; once the tree marks its 400th birthday, it is known (and sometimes scheduled) as ancient. The yew tree is generally much older than the oak (up to 5,000 years has been whispered), but the age of the yew is much harder to gauge because of the growth habit which twists and twines, pushing out new shoots and discarding the old as it sees fit.

Acorns were once upon a time used as food, and though this fell by the wayside as we learned to grow grain, they were still used during times of scarcity. Oak crowns were worn when the grain was harvested as a thanks to the earlier ways. As foraged food goes, acorn flour is OK, although I am sure that most foragers would agree that quite a lot of leaching is needed to make the mouth-puckering tannins of the ground acorns palatable. However, if you are in the USA, find a white oak (*Quercus alba*) and use those acorns instead. The tannins are not nearly as harsh.

Oak Gall Ink

My own favourite use for oak trees is to make ink.

To do this, first you need to find oak galls, which are the growths on leaves and twigs made by oak gall wasps. An oak gall is usually the size of a child's marble, brown and with a tiny hole. Look down as well as up; sometimes the galls hide in the leaf litter underneath the tree. If the gall doesn't have the little hole, leave it alone as this means the wasp larva is still growing. Gather as many galls as possible.

In the meantime, soak a few rusty nails in some vinegar in a tub, leaving the tub for a couple of weeks with a piece of card loosely on top (to allow it to breathe).

Then, grind the galls as best you can to make a powder and add the liquid from the nails; 50:50 is a good ratio. When you come to try writing with the ink, do not use a good pen as it will be ruined forevermore. Use a stick or a bamboo pen. Oak gall ink is indelible, even used for the signing of the Magna Carta in 1215.

CHAPTER 4

NINE BYGONE PLANTS OF THE MEADOWS

Nine Bygone Plants of the Meadows

A meadow is a large, open tract of land covered in native herbs, grasses and non-woody wildflowers. It is left to grow through the spring and summer months before the grass is cut in the later part of the summer, for hay to feed the animals in winter, and then grazed until the ground becomes too wet.

Natural meadows, largely untouched by us, are rare. If we believe that biodiversity is important, then we need to protect meadows, wherever they are on the planet. One single meadow can be home to at least 100 different wildflower species as well as numerous other forms of wildlife.

And here's something you need to know. The UK was once covered in meadows. But *97 per cent of British meadows have disappeared since 1930*. This is why I opened this chapter with the word "bygone".

The truth is that this habitat will never come back. And that is mainly down to us, as in Joni Mitchell's song "Big Yellow Taxi", not knowing what we have until it's gone.

We humans seem to like to fill in gaps, and we love to build. Meadows might look like empty spaces, not useful, but this is not the case. Although we are, in general, much more aware of our natural environment than we used to be, we need to think in a radically different way before it's too late. Hate to tell you this but I can't see that this will change any time soon, and that's why I wanted to include meadows in this book.

At the time of writing, I am reading about a situation in Philadelphia, USA. The Franklin D. Roosevelt Meadows is the only green space left in south Philadelphia. Already 50 irreplaceable ancient and heritage trees have been felled in the park along with hundreds of others, and much of the former meadows have been left a wasteland, with artificial grass actually replacing the real thing. Does this make any sense at all? During a time when our mental health is chronically endangered, our beautiful natural places are needed more than ever.

Let's see what we could be missing, wherever there are meadows. What might we find? And what might we forage?

1. Meadowsweet

(Filipendula ulmaria)

Other common names suggest meadowsweet's habitat – queen of the meadow, queen of the ditch – and its frothiness – bridesmaids, bridewort. "Meadow" evokes not only the place the plant grows but also the heady scent of mead.

HOW TO IDENTIFY MEADOWSWEET

This plant is decidedly frothy! The stems are tall, up to 1.2m (4ft), with dark green foliage and cream-coloured white petals. Found in ditches, on the edges of fields and roads, and, of course, in meadows in the midsummer or early autumn months, from June to September (sometimes beyond), beautiful meadowsweet is often smelled before it can be seen, the scent carried on the breeze, especially on a warm day. The scent can be overpowering, especially if you dry the tiny petals indoors. Your house will smell of marzipan, possibly with a headache attached, so beware. Also, if you suffer from hay fever, keep those billowy blossoms outdoors.

ALL ABOUT MEADOWSWEET

In the days of Elizabeth I, meadowsweet was one of the fragrant plants used as a strewing herb. The fresh blossoms were scattered over the stone flags so that the usual foul stench would be lessened.

The Druids are said to have loved meadowsweet, along with water mint (*Mentha aquatica*) and vervain (*Verbena officinialis*), and used it as a remedy for fevers and an ingredient in wine, beer and vinegar. As far as I'm concerned, the addition to vinegar is the best, giving a full flavour, tricky to guess. The Anglo-Saxons, it is said, also used the herb. During World War I, the Board of Agriculture listed the plant as "wanted by herbalists and pharmacists". Folk healers used the plant to treat anaemia, and an infusion of the leaves is still used to relieve a headache.

Where I live, in an unspoiled part of Wales, there was a superstition until the 20th century that if you fell asleep breathing the scent of meadowsweet, you might not see the morning. Quantities of meadowsweet have been found in Bronze Age burials, telling us the plant was possibly used in funerary rites, or to sweeten the corpse. We will never know. What we do know is that meadowsweet contains salicylic acid, the active ingredient in aspirin, an effective painkiller. In 1897, the chemist Dr Felix Hoffman was the first person to synthesize the drug; he used meadowsweet.

Meadowsweet Syrup (or Ice Pops)

You will need:

100g/3½oz freshly gathered meadowsweet blossoms (with the blossoms open)
0.5–1kg/1lb 2oz–2lb 4oz cane sugar, depending how sweet you like it
2 unwaxed organic oranges, thinly sliced
Lollipop moulds, if making ice pops

1. Leave the tiny flowers in a bowl for an hour or so to make sure any little insects can fly away.

2. Give each stem a good shake into a bowl and strip off the stems as they will be very bitter. Don't rinse the flowers as this is where the flavour is. (I know this might sound strange. Don't worry.)

3. Bring 2 litres/70fl oz/8½ water to a boil. Add the sugar and stir thoroughly to dissolve.

4. Take the pan off the heat and add the flowers. Make sure the flowers are completely submerged, then add the orange slices and stir again.

5. Put the lid on the pan and allow to steep overnight. The flavours will do a happy dance.

6. Next day, if you want a clear drink, let it drain naturally through a fine-meshed sieve or a muslin; if you want a cloudy drink, press the liquid through the sieve or cloth.

7. Store in the refrigerator in clean, sterilized glass bottles with screw-top lids. This is a cordial, so add water or ice as you prefer to serve. You can also pour the liquid into lollipop moulds and freeze for meadowsweet ice pops!

2. Pineapple weed

(Matricaria discoidea)

In *Matricaria discoidea*, we meet a relative of one of the original nine plants. Pineappleweed is also known as wild chamomile, although I would say the flavour is distinctly different from "normal" chamomile. If you are trying it for the first time, it's likely that you will be amazed!

HOW TO IDENTIFY PINEAPPLE WEED

This is a miniature sort of plant, which generally surprises even the most hardened of foragers. At full height it gets to 40cm (16in), and has a cone-shaped flower with tiny florets that are each not much bigger than the head of a pin. The stem and feathery leaves have the same pineappley flavour and scent.

If you want to look for pineappleweed, keep your eyes peeled for grassy places where there's regular foot or vehicle traffic, such as busy driveways or farmyards, or a track through a meadow. Pineappleweed loves to be pressed into the soil, where the seeds will then proliferate joyfully.

ALL ABOUT PINEAPPLE WEED

In terms of medicinal use, this plant has many of the benefits that you would expect from its cousin, chamomile. It's good as a digestive, or in cases of insomnia (used as a night-time drink) and is also used to numb pain. For example, it can be used on insect stings quite successfully, something I discovered by accident when a foraging client was stung by a wasp.

Here's another foraging story about pineappleweed. A little time ago I was asked to take out a small foraging party with a specific task in mind. My lovely clients were four girls, sisters aged from five to eleven, plus their mum. The idea was to honour their grandma, who had died, by raising funds for a charity. They wanted to be able to make something that they could sell, preferably food or drink.

The group was staying in a hotel that boasted a large wildflower meadow, including an area where people were allowed to walk about, not among the flowers, but along a designated track . . . which was teeming with pineappleweed! It was perfect, and I showed them how to make a cordial.

Later, I contacted the girls to see how it went. In the video call, they showed me the first banner that they had made, which said "Pineappleweed Cordial".

"No," the mother had suggested. "You can't possibly think that people will buy something called a 'weed'. Call it 'Wild Pineapple' instead."

She was quite right, and the girls sold out.

Wild Pineapple Cordial

You will need:
300g/10½oz
pineappleweed tops
300g/10½oz sugar

Here is that winning cordial!

1. Wash the pineappleweed tops and stems thoroughly, making sure that any muddy bits are discarded.

2. Bring 850ml/30fl oz/3½ cups water to the boil, then add the pineappleweed and leave for an hour or so, to let the herb infuse. If you prefer a less sugary taste, add more water.

3. Strain the liquid through a fine-meshed sieve or a muslin and bring to the boil again, adding the sugar to the boiling infusion and letting it disolve fully. Allow to cool and serve with fizzy water or crushed ice.

3. Red Clover

(Trifolium pratense)

Clover fits beautifully into this chapter about meadows but it is also happy to roam further afield. There are some 300 species of clover all over the world. Folk names of this humble weed include beebread, honeysuckle clover, meadow trefoil, shamrock and red clover (*Trifolium pratense*); this last is the one that we are looking into here.

HOW TO IDENTIFY CLOVER

Clover is one of those rather overlooked plants, so common that we hardly regard it at all. Red clover is a short little plant with pink to reddish-purple flowerheads, and leaves with three distinct "petals", each with a separate "line" like the gutter of a tiny book.

ALL ABOUT CLOVER

On the Greek island of Kos, there's a formula carved onto the Temple of Asclepius that mentions clover along with thyme and fennel. And Pliny the Elder reported that drinking wine mixed with 20 clover seeds would neutralize the venom of scorpions and snakes. It was believed that you would never find snakes in a meadow full of clover.

If you are still not enamoured of this charming plant, go find a pack of cards and you'll see that the clover has a huge part to play, being used to illustrate Clubs. This brings us to clover's role as a lucky charm.

Once upon a time, clover was scattered over graves as a symbol of resurrection; it's also a symbol of the Holy Trinity. St Patrick used a shamrock (which may have been red clover or another species) to explain the mystery of the Holy Trinity; on his saint day on 17 March, the shamrock motif is everywhere you look. Clover flowers and leaves also close in bad weather and open in good, so were used as a predictive tool.

The four-leaf clover is still the ultimate lucky charm, although there can, apparently, be too much of a good thing, and clovers with seven or more leaves are believed to actually have a reverse effect. One time, I found a nine-leaved clover, but so far everything has been fine.

Not used as much medically as in former times, red clover flowers are still used as an expectorant, as a treatment for gout and for some skin disorders.

Not so very long ago, children on the way to school would eat red clover (the flowers and the leaves!). It's flavoursome, surprisingly chewy, even filling, almost; just make sure there are no insects inside before you chomp down. If it's a nice day and you see bees on the ground eating the flowers, it means that conditions are perfect for a delicious snack, the taste of the nectar enhanced by the warmth of the sun.

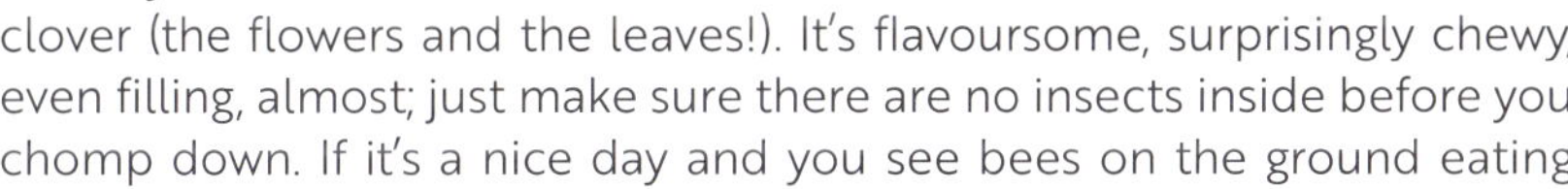

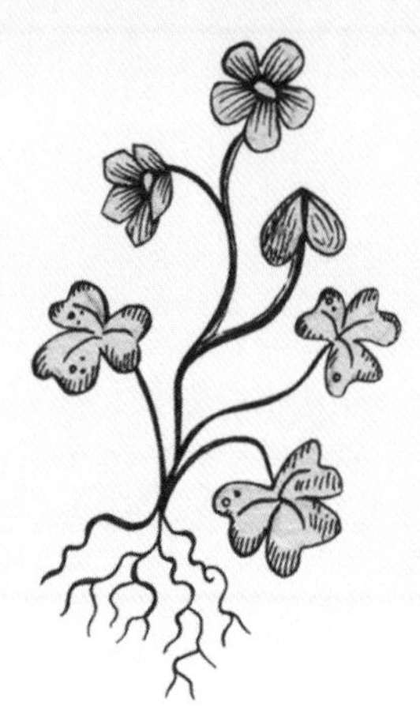

Forager's Choice by Lady Danni, aka the Landed Gentress

Lady Danni, aka the Landed Gentress, is a forager, educator and activist, a passionate advocate of the Save the Meadows grassroots coalition opposing the privatization and destruction of the Franklin D. Roosevelt Meadows urban woodland in Philadelphia (see page 87). You know when you "know" someone immediately, even though you have never met? For me, she's one of those. She's a force for good but not to be messed with!

When I show novice foragers wood sorrel for the first time, many assume it's clover because of its three leaves. But if you look closely, you'll see this three-leaved plant bears heart-shaped, rather than round, leaves. Once they try it, someone will usually remember tasting it as a child and calling it "sour grass". That sour taste from the plant's oxalates imparts a lemony flavour; the herb can be used in fish or chicken dishes, or to make a foraged lemonade or a condiment much like capers.

Lady Danni's Wood Sorrel Lemonade

Wood sorrel is a refrigerant, helping naturally to cool the body, and the sharp burst of tartness works as a sialagogue, which makes your mouth water, so enjoying this lemonade on a warm day can quench a dry mouth while refreshing your body.

First, gather two large handfuls (2 cups or 30g/1oz) or more of wood sorrel (the more you use, the more lemony it will taste). Remove any damaged leaves or stems and allow any insects to escape before rinsing. Bring 950ml/33fl oz/4 cups water to a boil, then add the wood sorrel. Allow to steep for 10 minutes before straining. Sweeten to taste with honey or sugar, then allow to cool and chill or pour over ice to enjoy.

Lady Danni's Wood Sorrel Capers

When wood sorrel produces seedpods, I love collecting them and using them as a foraged version of capers. I look for plants with loads of seedpods and harvest the larger ones that are about the length of your thumbnail. I usually take a minimum of three dozen, but if you can get enough to fill your jar by at least half before pouring over the mixture that's good.

Remove stems and wash. In a nonreactive pot, combine 125ml/4fl oz/½ cup vinegar and 60ml/2fl oz/¼ cup water. Add 1 teaspoon of salt. Bring to a boil to dissolve the salt. Place your sorrel pods into a clean, sterilized 225g/8oz jar and pour over the solution.

The capers will keep in the refrigerator for several months; to preserve them for longer, you can process the jar in a hot-water bath. Make sure there is about 1.25cm/½in headspace between the contents of the jar and the lid, seal and leave in boiling water, covered by at least 2.5cm/1in water, for about 20 minutes.

If I make the capers early in the season, I simply add more pods as I find them to the brine jar and enjoy them in fish or chicken dishes, salads or as an unexpected foraged treat on a charcuterie or cheese board.

You can use this same method with dandelion buds, which will give you a slightly bitter flavour instead of the lemony bite of wood sorrel.

4. Cowslip

(Primula veris)

The cowslip is one of the prettiest flowers. Also called the cowslip primrose or common cowslip, this is a true meadow flower, sharing space with its cousin, the primrose (*Primula vulgaris*). The name of the plant isn't quite as lovely as you might think; it means "cow slop". You will have to guess why. More bucolic names include key of heaven and herb Peter, as well as (in Devon) titsy totsy and (in Lincolnshire) milk maidens. The cowslip is a common sight in parts of the USA, including meadow environments, naturalizing in clumps. It is likely that European settlers brought it, either deliberately or by accident, via the seeds stuck in their boots.

HOW TO IDENTIFY COWSLIP

Both cowslip and primrose sneak into other areas, such as woodlands, verges and, in the case of the primrose, the wilder parts of a garden. If you're not certain of the differences between the two, know that the primrose has a short single stalk, whereas the cowslip has tall stems with clusters of small, bell-like yellow flowers.

ALL ABOUT COWSLIP

For pollinating insects this flower is very useful, opening before many others and therefore providing an early source of pollen and nectar for bees and butterflies. You can sometimes see those early bees blinking in the sun on the cowslips, looking a little dazed.

We may often overlook the cute little cowslip, but here's how William Shakespeare described it in *A Midsummer Night's Dream*:

> *"And I serve the Fairy Queen*
> *To dew her orbs upon the green.*
> *The cowslips tall her pensioners be;*
> *In their gold coats spots you see,*
> *Those be rubies, fairy favours;*
> *In those freckles live their savours.*
> *I must go seek some dewdrops here*
> *And hang a pearl in every cowslip's ear."*

An interesting folk name is palsy wort, which tells us that the plant would, at one time, have been used in the case of involuntary tremors, but of which kind, we do not know. We do know that the traditional use of the flower was to help with sleeping, because of its sedative quality. We no longer use cowslip for this reason, possibly because the plant is not quite as common as you might think.

As recently as the 19th century, cowslips were an important part of the May Day/Beltane festivities, used to decorate garlands for the maypoles, girls' hair and more. It is said that the maypole tradition survived for some 2,000 years in some parts of the world. This ancient, mysterious and charming custom seems to be having something of a revival in Britain, with primary school children trying out maypole dancing in springtime.

5. Corn Poppy

(Papaver rhoeas)

There are more than 100 different species of poppy, which was native to Europe once upon a time and now has made itself comfortable in other places too, including Asia, Africa, the USA and beyond. The poppy that we are looking at here is the wild common or corn poppy (*Papaver rhoeas*).

HOW TO IDENTIFY COMMON POPPY

This is the poppy that is commonly found in fields and meadows, its pretty red petals bobbing in the breeze, just waiting for you to stop the car for a moment while you take a picture. The distinctive flowers with four petals grow from a rosette of lance-shaped leaves.

***SAFETY:* All parts of this plant can be toxic, so seek advice from a medical herbalist before consuming.**

ALL ABOUT POPPY

Although it's the opium poppy (*Papaver somniferum*) that gets most of the attention, the common poppy has its secrets to share, too. As a painkiller, the poppy has been used for centuries, soothing toothaches, sore throats, coughs, colds and more serious ailments. The fresh petals can be made into syrup or, alternatively, the dried petals used to make an infusion against many varied complaints. Most people would have had their jar of red poppy petals to use in this simple remedy. In latter-day herbal medicine, extracts of the red petals are used as a cough suppressant and also to induce sleep.

The poppy is a symbol of pride, probably because of the colour, and it is used in art to represent the Passion of Christ. Arguably, poppy is best known as a symbol of the battlefields, because poppy seeds grow rapidly in disturbed soil – almost overnight. The swathes of red flowers must have been an astounding sight. Waterloo, in Belgium, was the first such sighting of the common poppy, followed by the

battlefields of World War I and then, again, in World War II, The 1915 poem by John McCrae is a poignant reminder of the beauty of the red flowers in juxtaposition to the horror of war:

"In Flanders Fields
the poppies blow
Between the crosses,
row on row"

From 1921 onward, the proud little poppy became the symbol of the thousands of people who had died in the wars, commemorated every year on Remembrance Day, 11 November.

The poppy was once used as a protection from lightning, particularly with flowers gathered on the summer solstice. In the way folklore always seems to work, the poppy was also thought to attract lightning as well as keeping it away. It was said that "Plucked poppies make thunder"; if the petals fell off while being picked, they could attract lightning. This odd idea is reflected in some of the names of the flower: lightnings, thundercup and thunderflower.

In some places, the poppy was seen as a plant of misfortune. It was believed that any contact with poppies would cause issues with the ears and eyes. Worse, if you stared at poppies for too long, you could even run the risk of going blind, hence its folk names blind eyes and blind buffs. If this is true, I would be surprised, but I'm not about to try it, just in case.

6. Cornflower

(Centaurea cyanus)

There are over 700 species of cornflower, with a genus name of *Centaurea*, and the one we are looking at here is the annual cornflower (*Centaurea cyanus*). Indigenous to the Mediterranean basin, the cornflower boasts a multitude of names, some of which are shared with other flowering plants: bachelor's buttons, blue bonnets, blue poppy, bluebottle, ragged robin and more.

HOW TO IDENTIFY CORNFLOWER

Found in meadows, verges and gardens, this pretty little plant has pointed leaves. Some varieties of cornflowers have black or brown buds. The traditional cornflower blue of its flower is possibly the most beautiful blue on the planet, but the plant comes in white, pink and purple, too.

ALL ABOUT CORNFLOWER

Cornflower has been with us from at least the Bronze Age. These plants are wonderful for pollinators as they produce lots of nectar and are attractive to butterflies, insects and day-flying moths.

The Greeks and Romans named the plant *kentaureion* or *centaurea*, meaning "the plant of the centaur". This mythological creature – half-man, half-horse – was fabled to have an extensive knowledge of healing, and can be seen in the night sky as the Zodiac sign Sagittarius. The warrior Achilles, who is generally known to have used yarrow to staunch wounds (see pages 204–205), also tried to use cornflower; this didn't work, unfortunately. Interestingly, cornflower was once used as a disinfectant for wounds of the eyes.

And did you know that, when the tomb of Tutankhamen was opened in 1922, the blue cornflower petals inside had hardly faded, though they were left there sometime around 1550 BCE?

As late as the 1930s, people used to cover their eyes with the first cornflowers of spring in order to strengthen them. A similar idea relates to St John's wort (see pages 219–220), a little later on in the summer;

the charm goes like this: "Peek a boo, John's Fire, and strengthen my eyes". Interestingly, one folk name for cornflower is break-your-spectacles, and the plant was used as a disinfectant for wounds of the eyes.

Another old name for cornflower was bluebottle, but nothing to do with the fly. Nicholas Culpeper wrote, "The powder or dried leaves of the bluebottle, or cornflower, is given to great success to those who are bruised by a fall". These plant stories are charming and there is often more than a grain of truth in them.

The juice of cornflowers makes a good blue ink, and cornflower blue was used as a pigment for artists or painters, also for dyeing wool, foodstuffs and even champagne. In case you want to try the blue champagne, it fades fairly quickly, so drink up.

It's fun to go out one day and look for as many different blue flowers as you can see, noting how many different shades there are. You might fancy a little drawing, too. These sorts of activities are for everyone; as we get older we often stop doing the things that we loved as kids. Remember you are still the same person!

7. Evening Primrose

(Oenothera biennis)

Evening primrose is native to eastern and central North America and was introduced to Europe in the 16th century or possibly later. The abundance of folk names tells us that the plant is loved and revered. They include evening star, sundrop, weedy evening primrose, hogweed (meaning that pigs eat it), king's-cure-all and fever plant. It is in the same plant family as the willow tree; now you know this, you will immediately see the similarities in the leaves.

HOW TO IDENTIFY EVENING PRIMROSE

This is a tall plant, some 1–1.5m (3–5ft) or more, with up to four large petals and somewhat floppy lance-shaped leaves. The flowers are typically yellow but can also be pink or white. It comes into its own in the evening, when its fragrance is unmistakable. This intriguing plant can be found growing wherever it likes to grow, not always where you would like it to be; but it does like meadows and pastures along with other places where the soil is poor and therefore often neglected.

ALL ABOUT EVENING PRIMROSE

I love this plant so much. Aside from any other consideration (the baby-soft yellowness, the open cup shape like something from the Mad Hatter's tea party, the lance-shaped leaves), there is one more aspect that thrills me: evening primrose blooms in the evening. The flowers begin to open just as it is getting dark, in the twilight hours, releasing a magical aroma that doesn't smell like anything else, and of course every single nocturnal pollinator, including moths, love the scent too. Evening primrose is happy in the daytime hours as well, in case you were wondering.

Indigenous Peoples of North America (such as the Cherokee, Iroquois and Potawatomi) used all parts of the plant in various ways, including the roots of young plants and the leaves, flowers and seeds. Evening primrose is also used as relief from migraine, helps the female reproductive system, and can have a mild laxative effect.

Arguably, it is the oil of evening primrose that most people know about, generally found in the women's health section in health food stores. Many women use the oil as a way of mitigating the misery of premenstrual syndrome (PMS) and menopausal issues such as hot flushes, a nuisance that can make a woman unhappy at best. As with all medicines, make sure that you have all the correct information you need, from reliable sources such as a medical herbalist.

As an activity, I suggest you simply find evening primrose flowers. Then eat them. They taste lovely!

Evening Primrose

This oil can be used when cooking as well as for your evening skin care. It is incredibly calming, soothing and gentle.

You will need:

A 300ml/10½oz jar with a lid

A mild oil that's not too flavoursome (comfrey oil is good, although expensive) or rape seed oil

A handful of Evening Primrose flowers

1. Gather handfuls of Evening Primrose petals and leave them to dry in the sun. The petals tend to emerge in stages rather than all at once and so this way, you can gather as you go and add to the petals as they are found.

2. Once all the petals are dried, put them in the jar and add the oil gradually until every petal is submerged. Otherwise the petals may go mouldy.

3. Put the lid on and screw tight. The oil can be used immediately, but the longer you leave it to infuse, the more of the petal's calming qualities it will have. This will keep in the fridge for up to 6 months.

Note: If you simply cannot find the suggested number of petals, don't worry. Just do your best!

8. Thistle

(Cirsium spp.)

Part of the daisy family, thistles are among those plants that are often overlooked, a nuisance at best . . . unless, of course, you think they are beautiful. Let me see if I can persuade you to look again at this remarkable set of plants, found around the globe.

There are some 200 thistles to be explored in North America and some 60 or so in the UK. The meadow thistle (*Cirsium dissectum*) is becoming rare in some parts so it's best to play with the common thistle, aka *Cirsium vulgare*, also known as the bull thistle, spear thistle and Eurasian thistle, which is widely found in many parts of the world.

HOW TO IDENTIFY THISTLE

As this section is about meadows, we will begin with the meadow thistle (*Cirsium dissectum*). Growing up to a height of 80cm (31in), this species of thistle often plonks itself into the midst of the meadow of its choice, where both European goldfinch (*Carduelis carduelis*) and its counterpart, the American goldfinch (*Spinus tristis*), fill their little boots with its seeds. Each plant bears a single bright pink-purple flowerhead and its leaves are not as prickly as some. Common thistles (*Cirsium vulgare*) are larger and more spiky, with multiple flowerheads per plant.

ALL ABOUT THISTLE

You might be astounded to know that not all thistles are prickly, and, moreover, most species are edible, too, although, to be very honest, only the hardiest of foragers would want the tedium of processing them. If you are feeling overwhelmed by the number of edible thistle species, bear in mind that cardoons and artichokes are thistles, too, their spiky parts overlooked because of the edibility factor.

The thistle is the symbolic flower of Scotland, but the provenance of this is hazy. The thistle in question is the Scottish thistle, *Onopordum acanthium*. Ironically, this plant was introduced from mainland Europe, but the fact has been forgotten for some time and, as I am part Scottish myself, I don't want to muddy the waters too much. There are many different versions of the thistle story, but here's the most likely one.

For hundreds of years, Scotland was part of Norway. If you look at a map of both countries, including the islands as well as the mainland, you will see why. However, by 1263, it seemed that Norway was no longer interested in the smaller territory. King Alexander III of Scotland thought it might be an idea to buy back his homeland, at which point the Norse king, Haakon IV, decided he wanted to keep the Western Isles and Kintyre after all. Isn't that just the way?

In the summer of 1263, Haakon set off for the Scottish coast and ended up in Largs in north Ayrshire. The legend tells us that the Norsemen, trying to surprise the Scots under the cover of darkness, took off their shoes to make themselves as quiet as possible; however, they didn't count on the fierce thistles and one (or possibly several) of them yelled in pain, To cut a long story short, the Scots (who, presumably, had kept their shoes on, ready for action) were victorious and won the day. The thistle itself was hailed as the true victor, a wonderful example of animism in action.

Don't forget the value of thistledown for nesting birds. The "down" is the airy part of the thistle flowers that contains the seeds, often seen blowing in the wind and used by canny birds for breakfast, lunch and dinner for as long as the seeds remain.

Thistles have a long history of medicinal use, including for ailments as wide-ranging as sores and abscesses, bleeding, liver problems and dysentery. More recently, it's been rumoured that extracts of thistle might have a possible use for some cancers.

How to Forage Thistle

Common thistle is quite invasive, and keeping it under control can be a Sisyphean task. Foraging thistle, therefore, has the benefit of also reducing it, one plant at a time. Here's how to do it.

1. Dig up the plant with its roots in spring or autumn, and take a moment to admire the beauty of its architectural shape. Choose as large a specimen as possible as you might as well take enough to eat.

2. Using thick gloves (not thin) remove the outer spines and leaves with a sharp knife.

3. The leaves also have sharp spines, so you will need to remove these too. If you have a good peeler, this will make life easier.

4. You should, by now, have both roots and stalks. Peeled stalks can be eaten either raw or cooked; blanch them if they're stringy. The best part is the root, which can be as tasty as a young carrot.

Foraging ideas like this are great fun, and it's a good idea to have a go at trying lots of them. You might only do something like this rarely, but it's the knowing that you can do it if you want to that's the real fun.

9. Buttercup

(Ranunculus spp.)

The name *Ranunculus* is Latin for "little frog", possibly a reminder that the flower likes to be in water (and can be regarded as a pest for those who prefer an orderly garden). The buttercup genus is huge, including some 1,750 or so cousins.

HOW TO IDENTIFY BUTTERCUP

Buttercup species can be small and also tall; its shining yellow petals and green filigree leaves are distinctive.

***SAFETY*: All species of buttercup – and all parts of the plant – are toxic for cattle, horses and humans.**

ALL ABOUT BUTTERCUP

This is one of the few plants in this entire book (see also pages 156–157 for the hemlock family) that has nothing for humans to eat. For such a well-known and much-loved little weed, the buttercup is also surprisingly devoid of folklore. I wanted to highlight the fact that not everything is for us. But we do reap benefits from buttercups in the pollinators that help us to survive. So it seems only polite to say a proper "hello". That, and the fact that there is much more to them than you might realize.

A lesser-known fact about the buttercup is that it has a nectar pool under the bottom part of the petals. Next time you find yourself among the buttercups, take a close look. This feature belongs to the buttercup alone; not even other yellow flowers have this particular superpower. It is a great bonus for insects and other pollinators.

Like many other flowers, the buttercup follows the sun and, in addition, the glossy petals throw out a vibrant light, a bit like a neon sign for a restaurant, to attract even more essential insects to their nectar feast. Buttercup's reflective cells are why the well-known kids' game of holding the flower under the chin, supposed to be a way of determining if someone likes butter, nearly always results in a resounding "yes"!

Although it might seem as though this particular meadow flower doesn't have much for us to be excited about, think again. Foraging is never just about us, and the story of the humble buttercup is a reminder of that. If there's a lesson in this, perhaps it could be to never underestimate the little things.

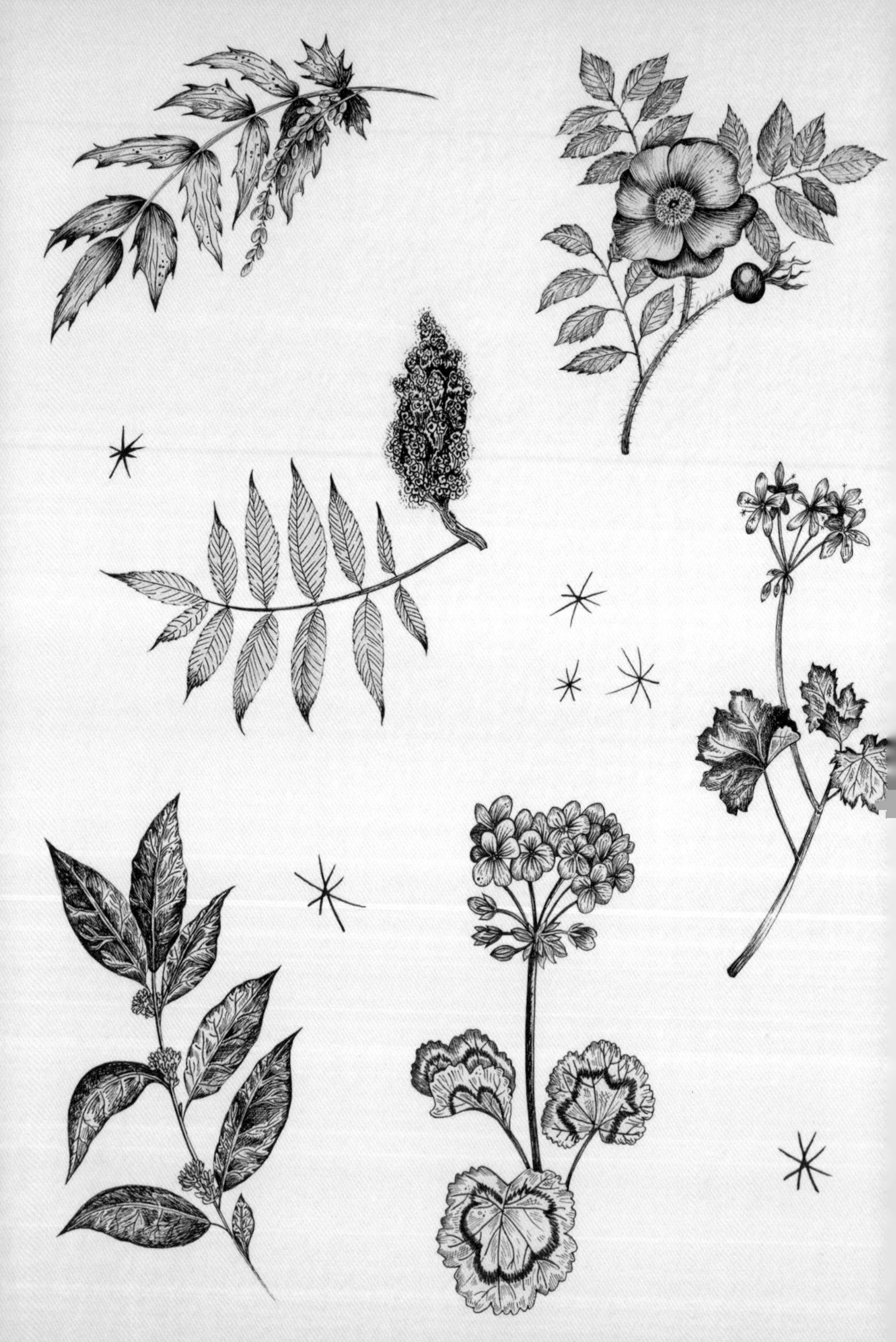

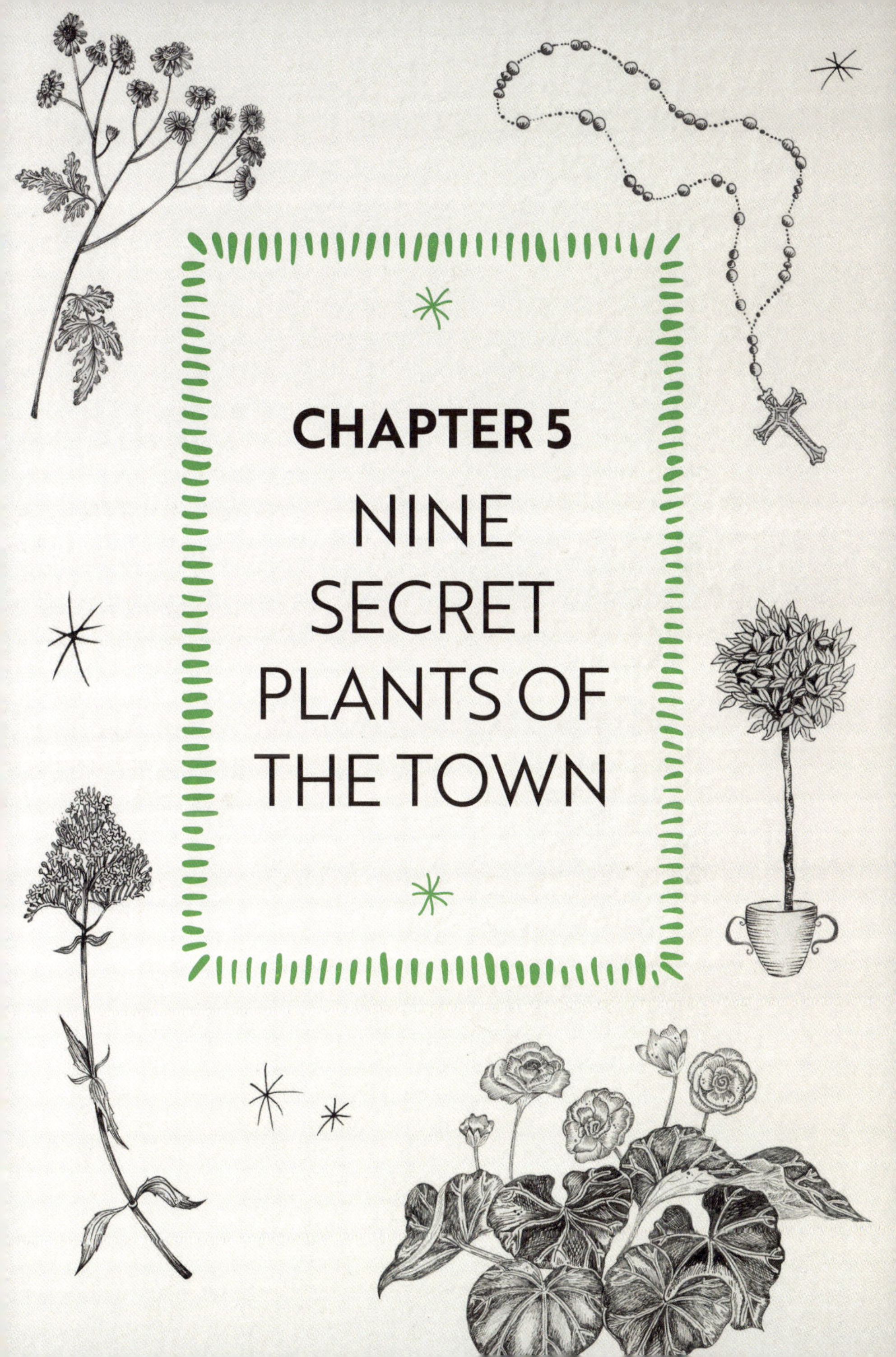

CHAPTER 5

NINE SECRET PLANTS OF THE TOWN

Nine Secret Plants of the Town

Does it seem weird to think about foraging in a city? Surely, the very idea of foraging in among the grub and grime is all wrong?

I can understand this wholeheartedly and probably wouldn't have attempted it myself until I was asked to take out a group in a decidedly urban environment quite early on in my own foraging journey. When I got to the venue where the would-be foragers were waiting, I assumed that we would hop into cars and share the driving. But no. The session was part of an organized "wellbeing day" and I hadn't realized that they expected me to rustle up edible plants and the rest amid a busy conurbation. It was the word "wellbeing" that threw me. It seemed like the very last thing that was appropriate.

However, after the initial shock, I remembered that I was a forager now. We are a resilient lot, and can make the best of a tricky challenge, and, apart from anything else, there was no choice without me looking like a fool.

These days, urban foraging is one of my most favourite ways to forage, mainly because I enjoy astounding my clients. Now, I make sure that I include this kind of foraging as often as I get the chance. There is a surprising amount of plant diversity in towns and cities. We (humans) have been explorers for thousands of years, inadvertently (or deliberately) shedding seeds from boots, giving free passage to insects, spreading fragments of flora picked up unnoticed from parklands, playgrounds, gardens and more.

Just make sure that you forage at a height that precludes dog or fox mess, and avoid areas of pollution (e.g. close to main roads) as well as municipal flowerbeds or school playgrounds. The grander hotels, contrary to what you might think, are usually delighted to support the novelty of foragers in their gardens, so long as you don't eat all of their beautiful flowers.

1. Rugosa rose

(Rosa rugosa)

There are 250–300 different sorts of roses, most of them native to the subtropical areas of the northern hemisphere. The rose, as an ornamental shrub, is the most popular and cultivated garden flower in the world today. Years ago, before I knew about *Rosa rugosa*, I would use dog roses (*Rosa canina*) in various recipes. But these little roses, while so pretty to look at in the summer months, are very tricky to gather, and the edible part is incredibly difficult to deal with. Then I discovered *Rosa rugosa*, also called the Japanese rose or beach rose, which are so much easier to handle and grow prolifically, suckering all over the place whether you like them or not and, handily, are found in municipal areas.

HOW TO IDENTIFY *ROSA RUGOSA*

Rosa rugosa is named for its rugose (wrinkled) leaves. It has straight thorns while dog rose's thorns are hooked, and its white, pink or purple flowers are larger than those of *Rosa canina*. It has a single layer of petals (as opposed to the multiple layers often seen in cultivated roses). In the middle is a small cluster of orange-red hips up to 2cm (¾in) long.

ALL ABOUT ROSE

The stories of the rose are endless – here are just a few of them. Some tell us that the rose was born from the foam of the sea, and white in colour because of it, but then Eros/Cupid splashed some nectar on the flower, turning it crimson. In other accounts, the rose is associated with daybreak, when Aurora/Eos, goddess of the dawn, opens up the portals of the day and strews all the colours in honour of the rising sun.

The flower is a symbol of mourning, too, the petals laid on the graves of the dead. The Romans ordered their graves to be scattered with the most fragrant rose blooms. In Islamic tales, the rose is said to have originated from the sweat of Mohammed. The dog rose was dedicated to Frigg, the German goddess of marriage and motherhood. Because the rose was sacred to so many belief systems, the early Christians initially regarded the flower as a suspicious heathen plant. However, this gradually changed, the flower or plant becoming used in a range of ways to mark birth, death and everything in between.

A rosary is a string of beads, with each bead representing a prayer. Rosaries are used especially by Catholic and Orthodox Christians, and prayer beads also feature in Hinduism, Islam and Buddhism. The name comes from the Latin *rosarium*, meaning "rose garden".

The hips are high in vitamin C and antioxidants. The leaves and petals can be consumed, too, perhaps by using them in an infusion or scattering the petals over a salad or stew.

How to Process *Rosa rugosa*

It's the ripe red orange hips that you need.

Squeeze to make sure the hips are ripe (they should have a little give), then take them home, slice lengthwise and freeze overnight (or for a few weeks if you don't have time straightaway). When you are ready, take them out of the freezer, let them warm up a little then squeeze; the pips will usually cling together and can easily be removed, leaving the tasty outer flesh to use as you wish in syrups, jams, jellies, teas and whatever else you can think of.

2. Sumac

(Rhus typhina)

Species of this interesting tree, *Rhus*, grow in many parts of the world. It is very ancient – sumac fossils have been found dating back some 49.5 million years. The name comes from the Arabic word for "red", so this is the "red tree". The dried fruit of *Rhus coriaria*, native to southern Europe and western Asia, are used to make the spice of the same name. *Rhus typhina*, the staghorn sumac, is the one often sought out by foragers.

There is a stand of sumac by the canal close to the next village along from mine, and another one a couple of miles further down, and two more of the trees growing in pots outside my garage. Not bad given that rainy Wales is not the most obvious environment for such an exotic plant!

HOW TO IDENTIFY SUMAC

The sumac you need is the staghorn sumac. Its red berries form fuzzy clumps, which sit proudly on erect branches and are fatter at the bottom and tapered at the tip, and are described as "candles" or "bobs". The leaves are particularly beautiful, long and sculptural, with a bonus that they change colour in the autumn, a firework of pinks, oranges, yellows and even purple. The tree can grow up to 3m (10ft) high.

***SAFETY:* There are also white-berried species of sumac in some areas; avoid these as they are toxic.**

ALL ABOUT SUMAC

In Native American cultures, the sumac is a symbol of protection and spiritual guidance.

The Greeks and Romans used sumac's red bobs to dye wool and tan leather. The fruits have a high vitamin C content and people once used them in a similar way to lemons, but lemons proved so popular, and so much easier to use. The red/pink colour tends to fade in time, as does the flavour, so if you wish to use sumac for its citric flavour – such as sprinkled into a pilaf, for example – make sure it's reasonably fresh.

I have found that sumac is easy to grow from cuttings, so if you can't find a local specimen you can buy one from a specialist nursery. Growing from seed takes so long that it's not really an option.

Sumac-ade

The fruits can be used to make a sort of lemonade, the natural acidic flavour as good as any shop-bought drink. This can be used to relieve a sore throat, sumac's natural antiseptic properties coming to the forefront.

To ensure the sumac "bobs" have a good, strong flavour, pick them in the sunshine (and not when wet) – you will need about four medium-sized bobs. Snap each little fruit from the stem into a bowl. Pour 1 litre/35fl oz/4¼ cups cold water over the top, then mash with a potato masher and leave for 6–8 hours (or overnight) before straining through a fine-meshed sieve or muslin. For a sweet drink, "sumac-ade", dissolve sugar to taste in boiling water, leave until cold, then add the syrup to the sumac liquid.

3. Red Valerian

(Centranthus ruber)

This is another one of the plants that is largely overlooked; it is so ubiquitous that we tend not to even see it. As you will have noticed by now, many of the plants that flourish in our vicinity were, once upon a time, native to the sunny Mediterranean climes; however, they tend to be happy wherever they land. (Please note that red valerian is *not* the one that is used as a sedative; this is *Valeriana officinalis* or common valerian, not quite so common any more, see pages 148–149.)

Red valerian has several wonderful names, including drunkards, sweet Betsy, kiss-me-quick, Jupiter's beard and keys of heaven.

HOW TO IDENTIFY RED VALERIAN

Small pink or red flowers grow in clusters on long stems (up to 75cm/30in), which also bear oval green leaves. Red valerian spreads enthusiastically and you can find it growing on walls and by railways, roads and pathways, as well as in flowerbeds where it may not be wanted.

ALL ABOUT RED VALERIAN

Red valerian flowers were used in country children's games, hence all the old-fashioned names that most kids today would probably run a mile from. I love the bygone charm of these folk names; my favourite name for valerian is probably kiss-behind-the-pantry-door with a runner-up of kiss-me-quick-mother's-coming.

Red valerian was first seen in British gardens sometime around the 1600s, wedging itself into the rocks and walls that it likes, and for that reason it is also called wall valerian. The walls of a cathedral, not far from where I live, is covered in the summer months with these fragrant red flowers, looking extremely pretty in such a place. If you want to get rid of the plant without using weedkillers, good luck; if you get the chance to see just how obstinate the roots are you will be astonished. Let's just say that this is a very determined plant for which the bees, moths and butterflies that it harbours are very grateful.

Red valerian is not known for its medicinal properties, but it certainly offers benefits to urban wildlife, as it grows where other plants might not want to and flowers through the summer, attracting many kinds of butterflies, bees and other insects. Its flowers are also a visual delight, brightening up the city streets. And if you've run out of leafy green veg, it can even be foraged! Unless you like extremely bitter flavours, it's the tender young leaves that you might like to eat, either shredded into the salad bowl or cooked as a vegetable.

4. Oregon grape

(Mahonia aquifolium)

American readers might know the origin of this plant's name. Oregon grape, aka *Mahonia*, is named after the horticulturist Bernard McMahon, who found it in North America when he was part of the Lewis and Clark expedition of 1804. The plant is the symbolic flower of the US state of Oregon.

I always find it odd that the plants that we often seem to use in "municipal planting" automatically look boring to the untrained eye. I think it might be because we expect "dull" and so that's what we see – prejudiced by our own low expectations. Oregon grape is really beautiful, however, and native to Asia and the Himalayas as well as the Americas.

HOW TO IDENTIFY OREGON GRAPE

Left unpruned, this plant will reach a height of 2m (6½ft), and is not fussy about soil, or sun or shade; a reliable plant and unremarkable until the bright yellow racemes of little flowers appear, with a heavenly fragrance, even better because the scent comes in winter. The leaves are glossy and prickly (like holly), and there are clusters of berries that are lightly bloomed and purple-black when ripe.

SAFETY: **Make sure the berries are ripe before you consume them. The plant belongs to the Berberidaceae family and so contains the compound berberine, which needs to be avoided during pregnancy and breastfeeding.**

ALL ABOUT OREGON GRAPE

Did you know that mahonia berries are edible? It's true! (So long as you consume them when they're ripe.) They can be as satisfyingly large as a blackcurrant, and are produced in bunches that are easy to harvest if you use decent gloves to protect your hands against the spiny-edged leaves.

The Indigenous Peoples used Oregon grape to treat loss of appetite; and there are many other medicinal uses of the plant. Some of these include the stimulation of kidney and gallbladder function, the improvement of the digestive system, a gargle for a sore throat, a laxative, a general tonic, and even a remedy for bloodshot eyes!

The main issue in harvesting mahonia is that birds of all kinds always know exactly when a berry is ripe and ready, and might get there first! You could possibly distract them with a bigger bird-table, or alternatively just leave them to it.

5. Feverfew

(Tanacetum parthenium)

The name comes from the Latin word *febrifugia*, which means "fever reducer". Other names include featherfew (probably a misunderstanding, but an apt one given its feathery leaves) and bachelor's buttons, a name that is used for several plants that have button-shaped buds or blossom.

This is yet another of those plants that is often passed by, almost as though it has a cloak of invisibility. If I am working with a group in an urban area, I will sometimes ask people to find plants that they might not have noticed before. Nine times out of ten, feverfew will be there. And nine times out of ten, feverfew will be passed over, despite being remarkably pretty and a lovely addition to a garden (where they will simply appear if they feel comfortable).

HOW TO IDENTIFY FEVERFEW

This is a perennial herb, a member of the daisy family (aka Asteraceae), as indicated by its daisy-like flowers. I often see these plants growing from walls as though they don't need much soil, and although the main time for this plant is supposed to be midsummer, I have noticed that they often stay where they are all year round. (Perhaps this is because of global warming – then again, cities are a lot warmer than the countryside so that could be the reason.) Feverfew grows into a small bush, up to 70cm (28in) high. The yellow-green leaves are quite pungent; people often say that it smells "medicinal", and I would agree with that.

SAFETY: **Avoid during pregnancy and when breastfeeding.**

ALL ABOUT FEVERFEW

The 1st-century CE Greek herbalist and physician Dioscorides used feverfew for "all hot inflammations", and it has traditionally been used in treating fevers, headaches and arthritis and for problems relating to menstruation and childbirth. In the 1970s, the City of London Migraine Clinic gave the plant its seal of approval, and a long-term survey of some 270 migraine sufferers began, recording the effects of self-medicating with the leaves. The response was remarkable; even after taking just one leaf per day, 70 per cent of the survey participants reported a significant decrease of migraine attacks. A double-blind trial ensued, with the end result that the active ingredients were isolated, and now the headache remedy can be bought over the counter.

6. Begonia

(Begonia spp.)

Begonia is one of those prim and proper plants that you might find on display in towns and cities, in elegant planters or hanging baskets outside shops or hotels or similar places to make the environment feel happy and pretty. You might also have them in your own garden. However, it's worth looking more closely at begonia, which in my opinion is a quirky and interesting flower. When not gracing swanky hotels, begonia proliferates naturally in the damp, subtropical places of Africa, Asia and south-central America. It was given its name by a French monk, Charles Plumier, a 17th-century biologist and explorer, and a clever man by all accounts who became botanist to King Louis XIV.

HOW TO IDENTIFY BEGONIA

Begonias have large, showy flowers in a range of different colours. Tuberous begonias (*Begonia* x *tuberhybrida*) grow from tubers. Wax begonias (*Begonia* x *semperflorum-cultorum*) have thick, waxy leaves and flowers that are much smaller and more discreet than those of the tuberous kind. Tuberous begonias have edible petals, stems and leaves, and you can eat the petals of wax begonias, too.

ALL ABOUT BEGONIA

You might be surprised to know that this flower is a good source of vitamin C; at one time it was eaten to combat scurvy. Although my foraging clients don't look as though they have scurvy, they are generally inquisitive enough to try a petal or two. The flower comes in all sorts of colours, but the general taste is a slightly sour, slightly sweet rhubarb flavour, a real surprise for anyone who has never tried it before. It's not often used as a garnish, but that's probably just lack of imagination on our part. I like to ask my foraging clients to try tasting unexpected plants and sharing these sorts of surprises with them!

In Chinese herbal medicine, begonia once had a range of medicinal uses and was applied in a variety of ways, including a disinfectant for wounds, to treat ailments of the kidney, and even to calm the pain of toothache.

You can use begonia petals in the same way as you would any edible plant petal: in salads, for example, or as decoration for a dessert or cocktail. The leaves of tuberous begonias can be treated as a leafy green veg and eaten raw or cooked, and the stems can be treated like rhubarb.

7. Sweet Bay

(Laurus nobilis)

You might think that the bay trees that often welcome us at either side of a hotel door, usually in a beautiful pot, would count for use in urban foraging, and I would definitely agree with you. But you might not know that to position a plant by a door is a reminder of an ancient and magical way of using the plant; a means of protection in which the plant itself was the magic. Ideas like this give me – and perhaps you, too – a real thrill of connection with the past and with other people who believe that there is more to "reality" than meets the eye.

HOW TO IDENTIFY SWEET BAY

Male and female trees have different flowers, both yellow, but the male ones are more yellowish with multiple stamens, while the female flowers are creamier with a green or red ovary and a single style. Small red berries on the female tree turn black in autumn (these are inedible). The leaves are dark green, oval and smooth-edged; tear one to release its distinctive aromatic scent.

***SAFETY:* Make sure you use *Lauris nobilis* as other varieties of laurel are inedible; the aroma of sweet laurel is the best identifier.**

ALL ABOUT SWEET BAY

The bay was a sacred tree for both the Greeks and the Romans. It was dedicated to Apollo, hence one of its names: Apollo's laurel. Because bay is a strongly smelling aromatic tree, the plant is also associated with purification rituals, intended to purge people, not only in the sense of physical cleanliness, but for spiritual cleanliness, too. At feasts held in honour of Mercury/Hermes, merchants and travellers would sprinkle themselves with a branch of bay that had been dipped in the Holy Spring of Apollo to cancel any mistakes made in the previous year. In times of plague, bay was set on fire and the ensuing smoke was wafted to get rid of noxious substances that might be lurking.

It was thought bay would provide protection against witches, demons and the more prosaic dangers of thunder and lightning. The Romans, too, believed that lightning would never be so rude as to strike the bay, so they planted the shrub close to the homes of emperors and priests. And so the tradition continued down many centuries, starting with ancient gods and ending at either side of a welcoming door in the 21st century.

One more bay anecdote: it was once used by the Priestess of the Oracle of Delphi, who chewed the leaves of *Laurus nobilis* in order to allow her to make her prophecies, to find out what the future held.

Bay leaves are still frequently used today, fresh or dried, to add depth of flavour to casseroles and other dishes. You could always plant a small bay tree outside your home, ideally one either side of the front door, as a way of symbolically protecting your property.

Bay Oil

Gather as many bay leaves (legally) as you would like to make a massage oil.

Half fill a jar with bay leaves, then add a cheap olive oil to fill the jar. Leave in a cool place for at least a year, then use as you wish, either as a massage oil or as a salad dressing

8. Geranium & 9. Pelargonium

(Geranium spp. & *Pelargonium* spp.*)*

Here are yet more common plants that are not common at all; like all our examples of mundane municipal gardening, there's more to geraniums and pelargoniums than meets the eye, as well as a good sprinkling of folkloric glitter.

Understanding which plant is a geranium and which is a pelargonium can be confusing. They were originally grouped by Linnaeus in the same genus, but are now treated as separate genera within the Geraniaceae family. Geranium is the botanical name, and also the common name, of one genus, while pelargonium is the botanical name and common name of the other. Geraniums are, in general, hardier, even able to withstand a mild winter and grow back every year, whereas the pelargonium cannot, so geraniums are referred to as hardy geraniums, and pelargoniums are referred to as tender geraniums.

You might know the hardy geranium by the name of cranesbill, because of the shape of the long, elegant seedheads. The pelargonium, too, has another name: stork's bill. Can you guess why?

These plants came originally from South Africa, taken to Europe by British colonialists; but geranium's popularity really took off when Thomas Jefferson got some plants from France and took them to the USA. There are many types of geranium. The "wild" kind is *Geranium maculatum*, a plant that extends from its woodland home into sunnier places too.

HOW TO IDENTIFY GERANIUM AND PELARGONIUM

If your geranium or pelargonium smells good, then it will taste good. Although the unscented kinds are not edible, nevertheless they have their medicinal uses, too.

Here, we are looking at the "cultivated" geranium and pelargonium species, to match the urban nature of these plants; of course, they started out as wild before being tamed into garden centre favourites.

The pretty, saucer-shaped flowers of both range in colour from whites to dark purple. The average height ranges from 15cm (6in) to 90cm (3ft).

ALL ABOUT GERANIUM AND PELARGONIUM

Geraniums are associated with all the good things: love, peace, happiness, fertility and even spirituality. I suspect that this is because of the scent. A tea made from geranium was at one time used in hopeful spells of love, and to aid conception. Your common or garden plant was once seen as something sacred, wonderful and magnificent, dedicated to the great god Odin, whose remit is that of poetry, wisdom and war.

In terms of traditional healing, the natural astringency of the geranium and pelargonium is said to help staunch wounds, and deal with kidney and irritable bowel issues. The Indigenous Peoples of North America used both plants to treat open sores and other wounds. They are considered antiseptic, too. In the UK, they were used to heal gout, and to stop bleeding after the removal of a tooth.

Did you know, in some parts of the world, these lovely plants were strategically put by windows, doorways and other prominent places, meant to ward off evil spirits and invite good luck and prosperity. If you have ever placed these plants in your home, perhaps you inadvertently are walking in the footsteps of ancient people

The pungent flavour and floral scents of the petals work well in cakes, meringues and other sweet dishes, as an ingredient or a decoration.

Pelargonium Sugar

Take a clean, sterilized, dry jar and into it tip 500g/1lb 2oz caster sugar along with half a dozen clean, dry pelargonium leaves, buried in the sugar. The scent will suffuse the sugar in just a few days. Although sugar is hardly a health benefit, as a once-in-a while sweet treat, made with flowers, this is something really rather special. Lovely for those who are good at making biscuits, too!

Incredible Edible: A People's Revolution!

OK so this one isn't a plant, but it's something that could make the world a better place and who doesn't love that? People who love plants tend to have an open and enthusiastic way of thinking, so it's likely that YOU, dear reader, will also share this ideology!

The Incredible Edible project began in the UK in 2007. It was founded in Todmorden, in Yorkshire, in an area that had once thrived because of the woollen mills, but those mills had closed down, jobs were hard to come by, the schools lacked resources and, despite the beauty of the grand empty buildings, the town and its people were suffering.

A group of some six or so mothers, worried about the future of their children, got together over a bottle of wine to see what could be done. There MUST be a way to bring the community together. What one single, simple thing could make it happen? The answer was . . . food.

Specifically, planting it, growing it and eating it. The ambitious community gardening initiative began with the intrepid mums planting potatoes in the middle of the night outside the fire station. Concrete tubs, previously full of rubbish, were soon filled with leeks and radishes. The idea was for people to turn unloved public spaces (outside the railway and police stations, along the canal towpath, the grounds of a derelict health centre) into free-for-all kitchen gardens, providing healthy food for the community, beautifying the environment and benefiting the wildlife, too. The failing school became home to a state-of-the-art aquaponics plant, providing fish, fruit and vegetables for the school canteen and educating the children about sustainable food production.

The idea spread to other British towns and then to different countries around the world, including France, Spain, Australia, New Zealand, South Africa, Argentina and Brazil. If you look at the Incredible Edible France map, for example, it is covered with red stickers showing that almost the entire country has embraced this groundbreaking approach to community self-help.

Foraging for healing herbs is not just about plants, or food, or ancient remedies, or folklore or mysteries. It's about people, making changes for the better, having an open heart and an open mind and wanting to make a difference.

If you are able to connect with like-minded people, then do it!

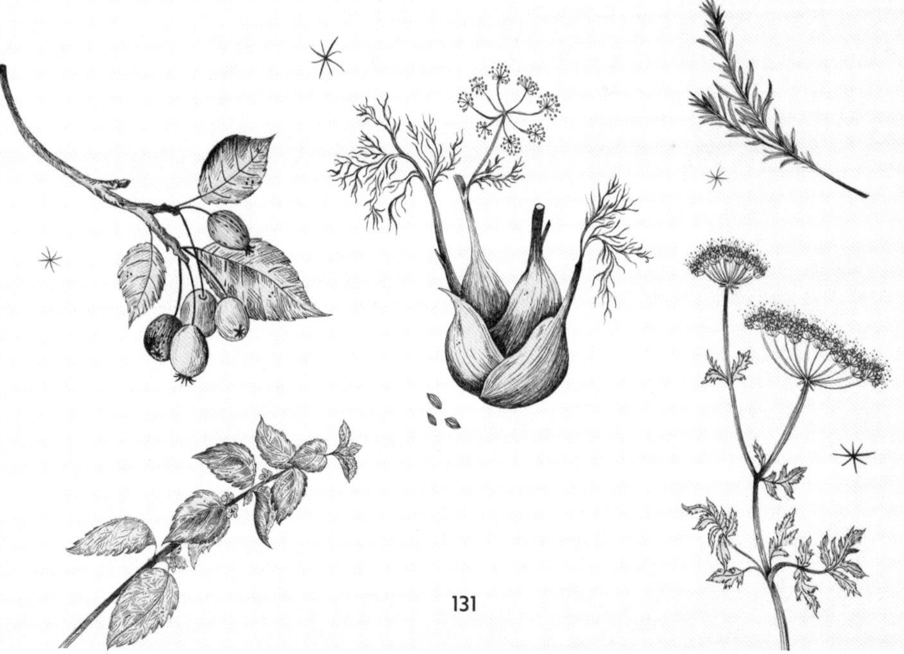

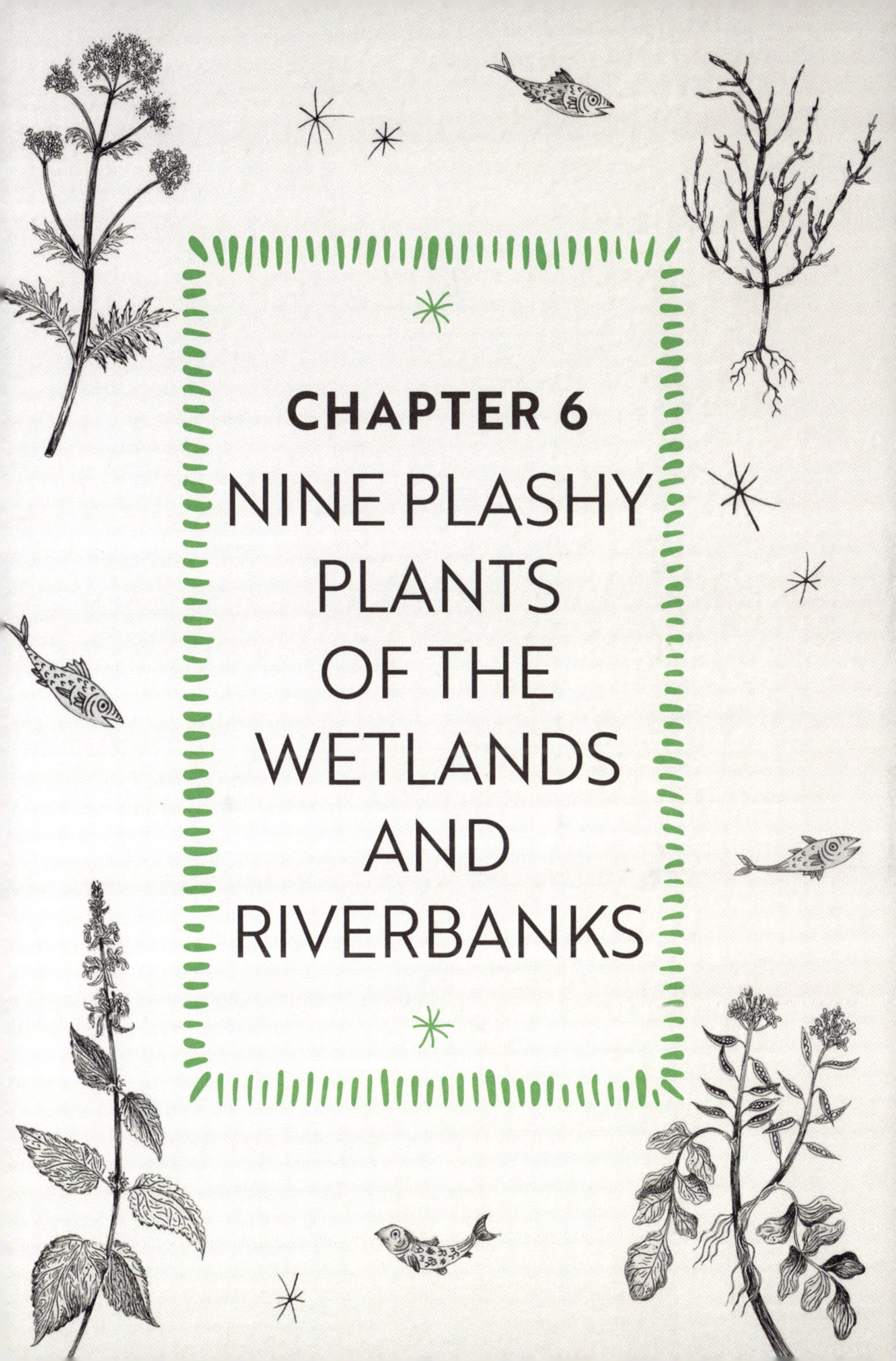

CHAPTER 6

NINE PLASHY PLANTS OF THE WETLANDS AND RIVERBANKS

Nine Plashy Plants of the Wetlands and Riverbanks

Plashy.

Indulge me for a moment. I love this word. It reminds me of paddling in the stream when I was a child, close to home, getting muddy and damp in water that was barely as deep as my ankles, a happy and reasonably safe way to play. Stamping in the water, falling over, laughing, trying to catch tiddlers with toy fishing nets but rarely having any luck. If we did make a catch, the sight of the little fish wriggling around, lost and terrified, was alarming, and they would be tipped back into the water as quickly as possible. Right now, as I'm remembering this, I can actually smell the claggy, muddy waters, very different to the scent of the sea, without the fresh smell of ozone. Isn't it amazing, how even just a memory of scent is so immediately evocative, years later?

Whether water is as shallow as the streams that I played in as a child, or as vast as the ocean, its living, moving beauty has a profound effect on us all; after all, it's our home, from where we once came. And where water meets the land – in the shifting wetlands, on a riverbank, in the shallow fringes of a stream – we find the boundary places, liminal spaces with a touch of the otherworld. Let's see if the plashy herbs that grow in these places might call up memories for you, too.

1. Mint

(Mentha spp.*)*

Mint and water have had a love affair, it seems, since the dawn of time. The plant and the water are inexplicably intertwined, and although mints are comfortable enough in a garden, they are really at their happiest when sitting in water. A member of the Lamiaceae family, mint not only has a wonderful scent and taste, but many medicinal properties, too. Mints include peppermint (*Mentha × piperita*), spearmint (*Mentha spicata,* the one noted for the fresh toothpaste smell), mohito mint (*Mentha × villosa*), also called cocktail mint or Hemingway's mint, in honour of the writer Ernest Hemingway, and Moroccan mint (a *Mentha spicata* variety), which is used for cooling drinks. Apple mint (*Mentha suaveolens*) features in cooking for its apple-ish minty taste. There are also countless hybrid mints that don't have names. But in any case, it's certain that mint won't care what name it's called!

HOW TO IDENTIFY MINT

We don't always notice mint as it sometimes hides under shady trees, but if you happen to tread on a clump straddling shallow water and soggy land, you'll experience an intense burst of delight, an unexpected shock to the senses. The leaves of mints can look different depending on the variety – apple mint has rounded leaves, for example, while those of spearmint are narrower, lance-shaped and with more jagged edges – however, as mint hybridizes happily, it's often impossible to determine a particular variety. The best way to identify mint is through the smell. It is very easy to grow, in fact it's considered invasive – anyone who has sown mint seeds directly into the ground will generally have plenty of it.

SAFETY: Not all mints are edible. The ones to beware of include hemp nettle (*Galeopsis tetrahit*), germanders (*Teucrium fruticans*), Corsican mint (*Mentha requienii*) and Japanese mint (*Mentha canadensis*). Pennyroyal mint (*Mentha pulegium*) was traditionally used as an abortifacient, so avoid if you are pregnant and also if you are not. Other, safer mints are available.

ALL ABOUT MINT

The use of mint dates back to the ancient Egyptians and Greeks. As you would imagine for such a popular plant, the folk beliefs about mint are many and varied. In Germany, it was believed that if cows drank mint, then the milk would not curdle. This idea was also held by the 1st-century Roman writer Pliny the Elder. Whether or not this would have worked, we don't know; however, it is the case that some mints (notably perilla mint, *Perilla frutescens*) is actually dangerous for cattle.

An old idea from Germany says that mint would refuse to grow in a household with a henpecked husband. In addition, mint was regarded as a deterrent to the Devil (we might assume that the Devil would not be keen to clean his teeth). In Belgium, mint was placed under the bed of a dying man, hence the name "old man's herb". Similarly, mint was crushed so that God would help someone who was dying, the lovely scent of mint both masking the stench of death while giving the dying person some solace. A sprig of pennyroyal was worn behind the ear to relieve headaches. Well worth trying.

Mint is known for promoting good digestion (think of after-dinner mints), as well as reducing nausea and helping diarrhoea and irritable bowel syndrome. Peppermint in particular, which contains menthol, is a good decongestant if you are bunged up with a cold – try inhaling it via steam or drinking peppermint tea.

Scrying with the 15 Herbs Charm

You will need 15 differing mints for this unique divinatory practice; the difficulty of finding so many could well be the reason why the 15 Herbs Charm is not more widely known.

Scrying involves gazing into a mirror or glass to open your mind to visions and new understanding; in this case it's done with the addition of the mints. I didn't think I could find 15 mints, but I'm lucky enough to have some great friends in a family business called Urban Herbs, who are always up for a foraging challenge.

Along with the mints I already had (peppermint, spearmint, mohito mint, Moroccan mint, apple mint, wild mint, pennyroyal mint), my friends Andy and Kate managed to source eau de cologne mint, pineapple mint, strawberry mint, grapefruit mint, banana mint, Tashkent mint, chocolate mint and curly mint!

Once you have your mints, find a clean bowl, add water to half fill it, then drop in a few leaves of each of the herbs.

Get comfortable, let the leaves settle, then ask your busy mind to turn off for a while and gaze into the water. Let your thoughts go, as you softly breathe in the aromas of all these wonderful mints, a sort of palate cleanser of the soul. As the chatter of everyday life clears, see what you find on the surface of the water, or what insights arise in your mind.

Scrying is not as easy as you might think, but in even just a few minutes you might be surprised by the ideas and observations that come to you.

If you can't find 15 different types of mint, then try this with just one or two! The mint will still smell delicious.

Forager's Choice by Andy Hamilton

Andy Hamilton is a renowned forager, who founded the Forager's Association, and a bestselling author whose works include *Booze for Free, The First Time Forager* and his critically acclaimed self-help memoir *New Wild Order*. He has kindly allowed me to select two of his brilliant foraging recipes from *The First Time Forager*.

Andy's Non-alcoholic Mint Julep

You will need:

Leaves from 3 sprigs apple mint, plus 1 sprig to garnish

Juice of ½ lime (25ml/1fl oz)

Ice

100ml/3½fl oz/scant ½ cup apple juice

1. Grab yourself a Collins glass (a long tumbler) and muddle the mint leaves with the lime juice. Top up with some ice and a spot of apple juice. Garnish with a sprig of fresh apple mint.

2. For a touch of foraging magic, you could add one of the botanicals, such as eucalyptus syrup – around 25ml/1fl oz per drink. If this proves to be too sweet for you, then you might wish to balance them with that magic cocktail condiment known to all bar tenders: bitters. I suggest that Peychaud's bitters will work better than the usual Angostura. However, these are 40 per cent ABV, so if you are avoiding alcohol altogether you might want to balance with a little more acidity, in which case up the lime or apple juice to taste. If you want to go the other way and add some alcohol, then the traditional recipe calls for bourbon instead of apple juice. Of course, as with most non-alcoholic cocktails, gin would work as an extra addition!

Andy's Lemon Balm-ade

My niece and nephew are confirmed coke heads; they love nothing more than a few glasses of the fizzy, sugary drink. Fuelled mainly by a lack of fizzy drinks (other than tonic water), I decided to treat them to something very different, which was sugar free and additive free too.

You will need:

2 handfuls of washed lemon balm leaves

Whipped cream dispenser

2 nitrous oxide (N_2O) chargers (8g/¼oz)

1 carbon dioxide (CO_2) charger (8g/¼oz) (optional)

1. Stuff a whipped cream dispenser or infuser with lemon balm leaves and top up with 500ml/17fl oz/ 2 cups water.

2. Seal and blast with two N_20 canisters. This will infuse the lemon balm into the water, and it can then be strained into clean, sterilized bottles or straight into a glass. It will be a little fizzy if drunk immediately.

3. For longer-lasting bubbles, add a blast of CO_2.

2. Wild Garlic

(Allium ursinum)

This is a stalwart of foragers and foodies. There are many different kinds of garlic, which is a queen of healing foods, so much so that I feel it should have been recognized in the original Nine Plants Spell. Here, though, we are looking especially at *Allium ursinum*, or bear's garlic. The botanical name is a nod to the possibility that bears, emerging from their winter hibernation and obviously hungry, would go looking for the garlic, rooting up all parts of the plant. It's hard to imagine this now, as bears have not lived in the wild in Britain for many centuries. Wild garlic is also known as ramsons or ramps, wood garlic, bear leek, buckram, cowleeks; place names such as Rams Dell or Rams Bottom indicate locations where wild garlic used to grow. If you see one of these names, or similar, have a look around – the plant might still be there!

HOW TO IDENTIFY WILD GARLIC

Wild garlic has a long growing season. It arrives at the tail end of winter, more or less, and is found in carpets in damp, shady places such as woodlands with running water. The young shoots are tiny, easy to crush underfoot, but soon grow to some 30cm (12in) or more. The leaves can look somewhat floppy and are smooth, widening out at the middle and tapering to a pointed top. The flowers follow, small and white, with six petals on a thin stalk. As the garlic plant ages, the seeds emerge from the flowers to make sure that there's enough for the next season.

SAFETY: **To harvest wild garlic, especially if you are a beginner, pick the leaves one by one and check for the distinctive garlicky smell. This is because the deadly poisonous lords-and-ladies (*Arum maculatum*) may be in among the garlic, particularly in the early part of the spring. In the early spring, the young leaves of lords-and-ladies look very much like those of wild garlic, but as they get larger and broader, they become easier to identify. Later in the year, lords-and-ladies has a bright red stem with matching berries.**

ALL ABOUT WILD GARLIC

Although we don't use wild garlic for medicinal purposes, we probably should. This plant contains much higher amounts of vitamins and minerals than clove garlic; in particular, its leaves have such high levels of magnesium that some herbalists call it "the Magnesium King".

Look closely at wild garlic seeds and you will see that there's a sort of "sputnik" look to them; they make for a great addition to a spice rack. Use them to add a garlicky flavour to salads, rice or pasta dishes, or sprinkle as a garnish. My personal favourite use is as a seasoning for a delicious wild garlic bread. Pickle the seeds like capers if you want to keep them for use later on. Wild garlic leaves can be kept in the fridge or freezer while you decide what to do with the haul.

The genus *Allium* really is something, containing not just garlic but also chives, leeks, shallots, onions and other foods. Let's quickly turn to the onion (*Allium cepa*). Although garlic is generally used to get rid of evil (in all its guises), the onion, too, has similar talents. Just like garlic, onions used to be hung over stable doors to protect cattle against troublesome witches. After a year, the onions were believed to lose their potency and had to be replaced. Also, onion juice used to be put into mole tunnels with the aim of chasing them away!

There was a report in an English newspaper of a woman's window hung with halved onions as a way of keeping out germs. This was in 1978, in the era of punk (I say this because it allows the juxtaposition of a window full of rotting onions and a mention of Johnny Rotten in the same sentence).

Onion Cough Syrup

This is a very simple recipe for a cough syrup. Why use a red onion? The idea is that the darker onions have more of the anthocyanins, which are believed to support your immune system in fighting off colds and even more serious conditions such as cancer. Honey, of course, is always soothing for coughs.

You will need:
1 large onion (red if possible), chopped
Liquid honey, as good as you can afford, and enough to cover the onion

Simply add the ingredients to a clean, sterilized jar, making sure that the honey covers the onion. Leave to infuse for at least a day (4 days maximum), then keep in the fridge until you need it. A teaspoonful should be enough for each dose. If you wish, add thyme, rosemary, sage or, indeed, any herbs that you have to hand.

Forager's Choice by Daniel Butler

Daniel Butler of Fungi Forays is something of a legend. Those lucky enough to go foraging with him will learn so much and feast on some of the best food that you could ever have. He is a generous tutor, too, one of the most generous I have ever known. His knowledge of birds and other wildlife is prodigious; I have to admit that I am totally in awe of him.

Daniel's Wild Garlic Naan

The delicate garlic/chive taste of the ramsons works brilliantly in this lightly leavened grilled bread, while a cheese filling keeps it gorgeously moist.

You will need:

75ml/2½fl oz/⅓ cup warm water
10g/¼oz sugar
2g active dried yeast
175ml/6fl oz/¾ cup milk, warm
150g/5½oz plain Greek yogurt
75g/2½oz butter or ghee, melted, plus extra for greasing, frying and to serve
500g/1lb 2oz strong white flour, plus extra for dusting
1 tsp bicarbonate of soda/baking soda
1 tsp salt
50g/1¾oz wild garlic, cleaned and shredded
140g/5oz hard cheese (Pecorino or Grana Padano), grated

1. Mix the water, sugar and yeast. When it starts to bubble, add milk, yogurt and melted butter.

2. In another bowl, combine the flour, bicarbonate of soda, salt and wild garlic. Make a well and slowly add the wet ingredients, mixing and kneading to produce a slightly sticky dough. Add more milk or flour as needed to achieve the right consistency.

3. Move the dough to a lightly greased bowl, cover, and leave in a warm place for an hour (or overnight in the fridge) to double in size. Knead lightly again on a floured surface, divide into 6 or 8 balls and roll out to form 2cm/¾in thick discs.

4. Lightly scatter the cheese over the surface of each disc, then fold over and roll again to produce another 2cm/¾in disc.

5. Dust lightly with flour to prevent sticking and pile on a plate, then cover to rise slightly. Heat a little butter or ghee in a large griddle or frying pan.

6. Cook on high heat for 2–3 minutes on each side, producing slightly blistered, puffed-up flatbreads.

7. As they come off the griddle, brush with melted ghee or butter . . . and enjoy.

3. Purple Loosestrife

(Lythrum salicaria)

It pays to have a scruffy garden, it really does. An unknown flower appeared in my messy vegetable patch, in which the snails and slugs were busy chomping on an "all-you-can-eat" buffet that had previously been marked for my own supper. They weren't in the least interested in this flower, though, so I thought it would be worth watching to see what it did. This was a few years ago, and now the flower has really settled in – tall, very elegant, the same height as me but with a real glamour, as though it moved in particularly grand circles. What a beauty! I'd never have managed to grow someone like this if I'd tried, I'm sure.

I discovered that the flower was purple loosestrife. The name comes from Lysimachus of ancient Sicily, whose name meant, in translation, "undo" and "war". Hence, "loose strife". The story goes that the king was the first person to use the plant to soothe angry horses or oxen by dint of putting the leaves on their shoulders so that the biting insects could nibble no longer. Therefore, the strife was no more.

HOW TO IDENTIFY PURPLE LOOSESTRIFE

The plant grows up to 1.2m (4ft) tall (though it can, as with mine, get even bigger), with spikes of small purple-pink flowers and long, slim, lance-like leaves that look similar to those of the willow, which in turn looks quite like rosebay willowherb; but they're not the same species, despite the similarities. This plant likes to hang out in ditches and other wettish places such as meadows, bogs, tidal estuaries, riverbanks and, sometimes, in fields and gardens.

ALL ABOUT PURPLE LOOSESTRIFE

Once upon a time, purple loosestrife was used as an insect repellent. The 16th-century herbalist John Gerard said of it "the smoke of the burned herbe driveth away serpents, and killeth flies and gnats in the house". Horses were garlanded with purple loosestrife to get rid of gnats and other annoying insects in the summer months. The leaves

of the plant, which have a high tannin content, were also used to treat leather in the tanning process. The same tannin made purple loosestrife a remedy for sore throats and similar ailments. Nicholas Culpeper backed this up, saying:

> *"It cleanseth and healeth ulcers and sores, and stayeth their inflammations by washing them with the water, and laying on them a green leaf or two in the summer, or dry leaves in the winter. This water, gargled warm in the mouth and sometimes drunk, cured quinsy, or King's Evil, in the throat. The said water applied warm taketh away spots, marks and scabs in the skin."*

The folklore of this purple plant is also fascinating. Magical powers were ascribed to it, helping people develop psychic and precognitive skills as well as calming an unruly horse and other animals. I have to say that this plant does look decidedly "witchy" in a Cruella de Vil kind of way.

In other matters, getting rid of the plant, once it is settled, is tricky as I found when I realized it was invading a little too much. The roots are iron-hard and very difficult to remove, so it's likely I will have it forever.

If you have a friend with horses (or if you are lucky enough to have one or two yourself), it might well be worth trying to use the leaves in the traditional way, that is, putting them under the saddle of the horse, particularly in hot weather, in order to keep the horse comfortable. If this worked in ancient times, there's no reason why it wouldn't work now.

4. Woundwort

(Stachys palustris & Stachys sylvatica)

There are two kinds of woundwort: marsh woundwort (*Stachys palustris*) and hedge woundwort (*Stachys sylvatica*). Other related herbs in this family are many and varied, including black horehound (*Ballota nigra*), ground ivy (*Glechoma hederacea*), and yellow archangel (*Lamium galeobdolon*), a plant that is either adored or totally unnoticed. However, it is woundwort that we are focusing on here.

HOW TO IDENTIFY WOUNDWORT

Betony (see pages 24–25) has a distinct look of woundwort; this is because they are close cousins. Marsh woundwort has pinkish petals, whereas hedge woundwort is darker in general, with darker purple petals. Both types of woundwort have hairy stems and heart-shaped, toothed leaves, and grow to a height of 1m (3¼ft). While hedge woundwort can be found in and among hedges, the marsh variety likes to have its toes in the water.

If we find hedge woundwort on a forage, I often ask people to crush the plant to release the scent. Mostly, plants smell nice. The inimitable stench of hedge woundwort is . . . uncomfortable, to say the least. Occasionally – *very* occasionally – someone might like it. Marsh woundwort smells much more pleasant.

ALL ABOUT WOUNDWORT

The good news is that both kinds do exactly what the name says they do, that is, staunch the flow of blood. Simply crush and apply to the injury, with a little spit (your own) for good measure.

I had reason to use marsh woundwort once. I'd been out gathering wild garlic, and when I got home I gave the delicious garlic leaves a good wash in water, then shook them dry(ish). Then I got my stick blender, did some blending, and then, with the blender still on, I accidentally blended

a not-unsignificant amount of my own blood in with the wild garlic. Luckily there were both kinds of woundwort close by, so I grabbed a bundle of leaves and pressed it to my arm, also holding it up to help staunch the flow. I still have the scar, actually. Don't do what I did.

As with betony, both woundworts can be used as a soothing tea. They have the same protecting and relaxing vibes. Marsh woundwort is considered effective in cases of eczema, dermatitis and psoriasis.

Marsh woundwort also helps to relieve menstrual cramps, and in addition the roots and tubers of the plant taste "peanutty". If you have a lot, try boiling them gently and you will find that they taste rather like bean sprouts; serve with olive oil or butter. (However, if you're not absolutely certain that it's marsh woundwort, leave it alone, as with any "not sure" plant).

5. Valerian

(Valeriana officinalis)

This plant might have been named after Valerius, said to be the first person who used it in medicine. Another possible root is the Latin word *valere*, meaning "to be in good health". Both explanations work well. Be aware that this plant has nothing to do with red valerian (*Centranthus ruber*, see pages 117–118), despite the name. Other names for valerian include all heal, great wild valerian, amantilla, setwall and capon's tail.

A funny thing can happen with plants, and my own search for valerian seemed doomed. Try as I might, I couldn't find it, so I stopped looking. Some time after this, I found myself in a wonderful nature reserve that had originally been an abandoned slag heap, covered over to make sure that the noxious chemicals beneath would never surface. This was in a former mining area; you would be astonished to see how nature can heal something so toxic in just a few years. As we strolled along, I realized that the plant I was looking at was the same as the valerian I had seen in books, acres of it, all in bloom! It was like meeting someone you'd made friends with online for the first time in real life.

Bizzarely, I found even more valerian in my next foraging trip; this time much closer to home. Then I found more, a mile from home, in a lane that never fails to help me. In this case, it felt as though the valerian was playing with me. This isn't the first time I have thought this about a plant.

HOW TO IDENTIFY VALERIAN

This is a tall plant of some 1.8m (6ft), with erect stems, pink-white umbels and a predilection for limestone areas. Generally to be found in marshy terrain as well as in dryer areas, valerian has a similar issue to hedge woundwort; that is, the smell. Personally, I don't think valerian roots are quite as whiffy as that. The flowers are particularly pleasing, a musky scent a little like vanilla; no surprises that it is used in perfumery. Valerian is even an ingredient in a perfume named Eau de Stilton, which, to be fair, is an unusual choice of scent to attract a mate.

ALL ABOUT VALERIAN

The herbalist Maud Grieve tells us that valerian was the plant "phu" used by Galen and Dioscorides, who recommended it as an aromatic plant as well a diuretic (phu indicated the disgust at the aroma of the root).

Valerian is known as a sedative, beneficial for anxiety. During World War II, when air raids were rife, it was prescribed to help people sleep, and a tincture of valerian was used for what is now called for PTSD. A good friend of mine that has suffered similarly swears by valerian tincture and recently started to grow her own herb. (If would like to try this, please consult your doctor and a medical herbalist.)

Cats generally go crazy for valerian. There's even a legend about the animals breaking into apothecary shops to steal it!

Valerian Tea

Use fresh or dried roots of valerian. If you are not experienced in foraging valerian, then buy the root from a reputable herbalist.

Place 1 teaspoon of dried valerian root or 2 teaspoons of fresh in a cup, pour over just-boiled water, then cool. If you wish, add cardamom, lemon balm or other relaxing herbs of your choice.

6. Marsh Samphire

(Salicornia europaea)

There are two kinds of samphire; the one that we are looking at here is marsh samphire. You can find it on the beaches, salt marshes, salty shorelines and mangrove swamps of Europe and the Americas. Names for this plant include sea asparagus, picklewort, pickleweed, mermaid's kiss, common glasswort or saltwort.

Marsh samphire is a succulent herb, built to retain water in times of arid conditions, whether in soil or sand. It is a pioneer species, meaning that it is the first to set up home (so to speak), enabling other species to prosper too.

HOW TO IDENTIFY MARSH SAMPHIRE

The plant can grow to some 35–40cm (14–16in) in height, with little branch-style formations that look a bit like a cactus, but without the spines. If you want to find it, keep an eye open in seaside areas from late spring to early summer. Don't uproot whole plants. (This is a courtesy more than anything; as of right now, marsh samphire is not endangered. Still, manners cost nothing.)

An easy way to get to know what this plant looks like is to find a good fishmonger. They will usually display their fish on a bed of marsh samphire.

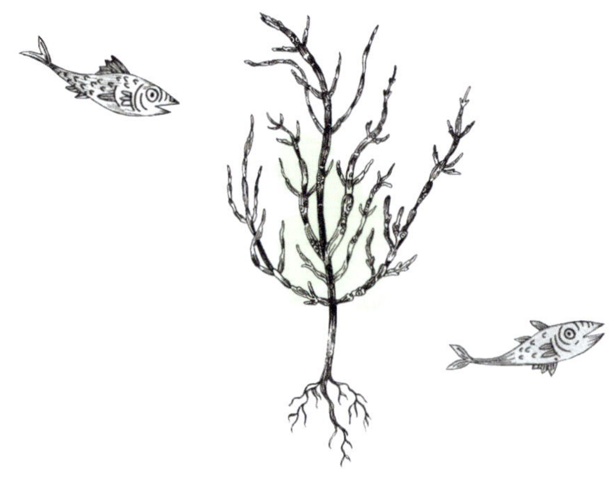

ALL ABOUT MARSH SAMPHIRE

The plant is dedicated to St Peter, the patron saint of fishermen. One folk name for this plant is saltwort, another is glasswort. The reason for the first name is obvious, but the second alludes to a less well-known use. Marsh samphire, along with other plants such as kelp, were used in making glass as well as soap, handy because marsh samphire is high in sodium carbonate ("soda ash"). In the 14th century, the trade was so busy that the makers located their workshops where the plant grew. Burning the plant released the sodium more easily than common salt; the resulting ash was fused with sand and then leached with lime water, either to make glass, or combined with animal fats to make soap.

Once used to treat scurvy, samphire is a good source of several vitamins and minerals, and has an antioxidant and anti-inflammatory effect. As a green vegetable, it brings a delicious salty and briny tang to meals.

Incidentally, my niece Lucy, when she was seven, loved samphire so much that she asked for samphire (and olives) rather than a birthday cake. I'm not quite sure what the other kids made of this.

7. Watercress

(Nasturtium officinale)

The name nasturtium might surprise you, as it is generally associated with a garden plant with bright orange, yellow or sometimes red petals, but it makes sense when you discover that *Nasturtium* comes from the Latin for "nose twister". Watercress is said to be one of the oldest leaf vegetables to have been eaten by us humans, and was originally found in China; it spread, as plants do, and now is found in many parts of the world.

HOW TO IDENTIFY WATERCRESS

Watercress can reach some 60cm (24in) in height with leaves either lying in water or standing upright; that water needs to be moving, for example, a shallow stream. The plant has small flowers with four white petals and small, rounded green leaves, which start out as circular and become lance-shaped with age. Its hollow stems are perfect for floating in water.

SAFETY: **If you want to try the plant in the wild, be aware that liver fluke can be an issue in wild watercress (although the tame stuff is OK). Do not forage if livestock are upstream, wash thoroughly and cook before eating. If eating raw, as salad, then add disinfectant to the washing water.**

ALL ABOUT WATERCRESS

Watercress is known, of course, for its hot and spicy flavour, similar in taste to wasabi and mustard greens, although not with quite the same sort of kick. In common with its other cousins, watercress was once useful in combating scurvy and, because of this, one of its names was scurvy grass (not the only scurvy-related name given to a semi-aquatic plant).

In the UK, the county of Hampshire and the St Albans area were once famed for watercress, because of the clear, clean chalk streams found in those places.

The Romans loved watercress, and thought that it would cure mental illness. Hildegard of Bingen, the 12th-century German mystical nun who was interested in just about everything, believed that steaming it and drinking the water would cure fevers. The Indigenous Peoples of America used it to treat constipation. It was also believed, in Ireland and Scotland, that it was possible to use watercress as a charm to steal the goodness from the milk.

Rich in vitamins (especially vitamin C) and minerals, watercress is considered nutritious, cleansing and detoxifying. One of the ancient Irish lays or poems called "Buile Suibhne" suggests that the watercress is not only a source of physical sustenance, but also of spiritual comfort and refuge:

"Watercress I pluck
Food in a fair bunch
Four round handfuls
Of fair Glen Bolcain"

8. Bog Myrtle

(Myrica gale or *Gale palustris)*

Bog myrtle can be found in many regions of the northern hemisphere, but is possibly one of the more unusual forageable plants. The preponderance of different folk names will tell you how respected it is: bog gaul, bog sally, sweet willow, sweet gale, Dutch myrtle and wild sumac.

I am lucky enough to have a largish stand of this plant just 8km (5 miles) away, settled by the only natural lake in the Brecon Beacons. The first time I encountered the bog myrtle was in the summer, and I had no idea what the glorious scent was.

HOW TO IDENTIFY BOG MYRTLE

As the name suggests, this plant needs boggy (acidic) conditions, such as an estuary. It is a deciduous shrub which grows some 1–2m (3¼–6½ft) high, with elongated, oblanceolate leaves in a neat spiral on the stem, and male and female catkins on separate plants. Bog myrtle is all about its scent, which has been described as sweet and resinous when the plant is in flower. The aroma from large colonies of the plant can travel for several metres.

ALL ABOUT BOG MYRTLE

Bog myrtle's scent is so wonderful that, in some folkloric traditions, the plant is said to be blessed; in Ireland, for example, it was once used on Palm Sunday in place of actual palms. The beauty of folklore is that one idea often appears alongside its polar opposite, and bog myrtle is no exception. It was fabled that the myrtle was once a large tree, but after it was used to make the cross on which Christ died, the plant was cursed, and rendered small and stunted as a punishment.

In medieval Europe, bog myrtle was a key flavouring in beer, before hops came into

use. Other key herbs in the "gruit" beer mix were yarrow (see pages 204–205) and mugwort (see pages 14–16). These days, there has been something of a resurgence of these old brewing traditions, and brewers in Belgium and North Yorkshire, at least, are making beer using these ingredients once more.

Queen Victoria was given a sprig of myrtle to use in her wedding bouquet, and the tradition of using the fragrant plant in royal wedding bouquets is still very much on-going.

The essential oil of bog myrtle can be used as a natural insect repellent. The young leaves can be foraged to make a fragrant tea, and the leaves also make a good seasoning (and are even used in perfumery).

Bog Myrtle Tea (with Wild Mint if You Fancy it)

As bog myrtle was once used as a sedative, try a soothing cup before you go to bed.

Pour boiling water over the leaves, let steep for a few minutes and strain.If you have mint, too, mix the leaves together for an unusual and fragrant drink.

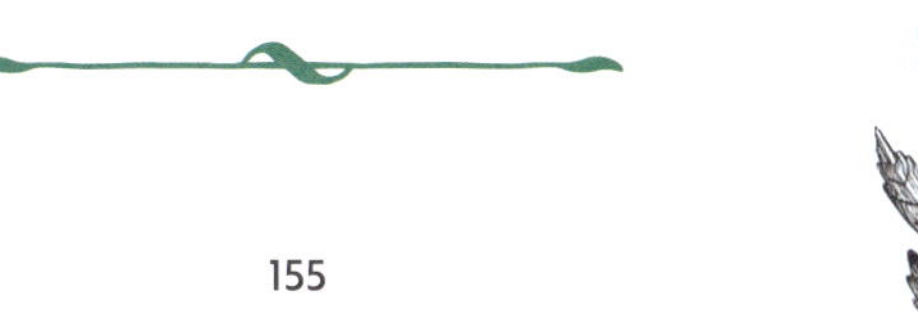

9. Hemlock Water Dropwort & Other Toxic Umbellifers

(Oenanthe crocata)

The name Umbelliferae was given to this family because many of the cousins have an umbrella-like top. It was changed recently to Apiaceae, but the term "umbellifer" is still widely used.

Here, we are looking at the more dangerous members of the family; although, be mindful that plants poisonous to us are vital to other lives. What's more, many toxic plants have medicinal uses, despite their toxicity.

The umbellifer or wild carrot family is vast, with over 3,700 species. If you love fennel, dill, parsley, sweet cicely, common hogweed, celery, Alexanders and actual carrots or parsnips, you are already cognisant of some edible members of the clan. The next four umbellifer plants are common but not edible, and are highlighted here for your safety.

1. Hemlock water dropwort (*Oenanthe crocata*)
2. Poison hemlock (*Conium maculatum*)
3. Cowbane (*Cicuta virosa*)
4. Rough chervil (*Chaerophyllum temulum*)

I will concentrate on hemlock water dropwort as it's the most common. Folk names include dead tongue, dead man's fingers, wild rue and dead tongue.

HOW TO IDENTIFY HEMLOCK WATER DROPWORT

Oenanthe crocata has grooved stems growing up to 1.5m (5ft) with smooth, purple blotches and parsley-like leaves. It gives off a distinct "mousy" smell. In full flower, it is beautiful, frothing with small white flowers in clusters. I have never seen hemlock water dropwort far from water, whether in a boggy meadow or by the bank of a small river.

SAFETY: Hemlock water dropwort, poison hemlock, cowbane and rough chervil are toxic to humans, horses and dogs. The motto here is "look but don't touch". As a general rule, if you are not sure of a wild plant, make sure you wear gloves while handling.

ALL ABOUT HEMLOCK

This plant family is beneficial to bees, wasps and other insects, some of which have a hard time due to habitat loss, exposure to pesticides and climate change. In fact, 2024 was the worst year on record in the UK for butterflies.

The fear that innocent edible plants – such as brooklime (*Veronica beccabunga*) or watercress (*Nasturtium officinale*) – might get mixed up with something more sinister is what's behind the Yorkshire saying "hemlock dropwort among the brooklime". It means something bad might be deliberately hidden.

Poison hemlock was the plant used to kill Socrates in 399 BCE. He was found to be guilty of "corruption of the young" and "introducing strange gods". The philosopher, knowing that he was effectively dead already, is said to have asked to determine the manner of his demise.

Hogweed (*Heracleum sphondylium*), is NOT toxic. But it looks very similar to its poisonous cousins so is best left alone. There are enough easily identifiable edible plants for foragers to be going on with! Hogweed seeds, especially young shoots, have a smoky, tart citrus flavour. I once made a hogweed and pineappleweed gin with the help of a local distiller.

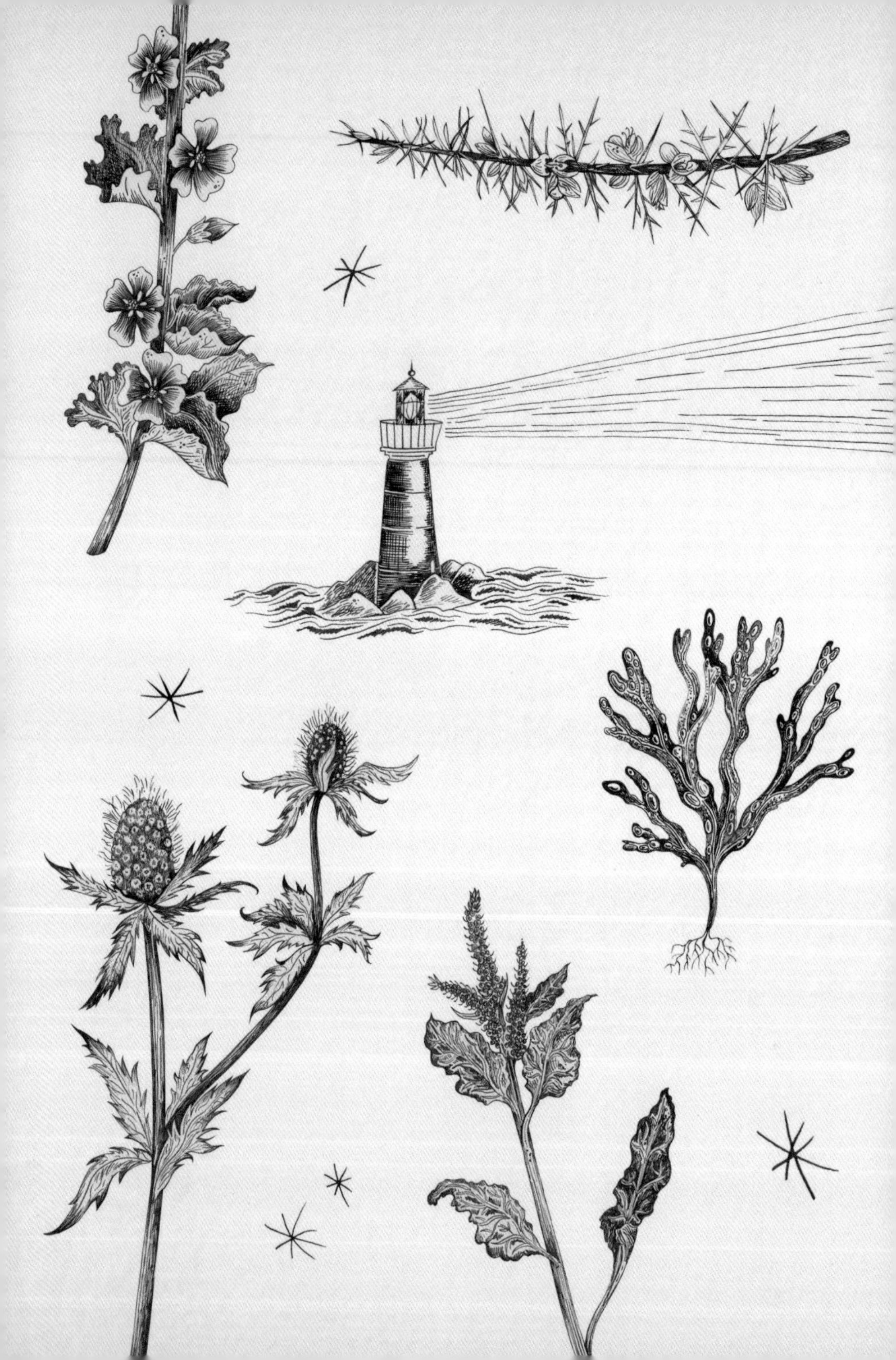

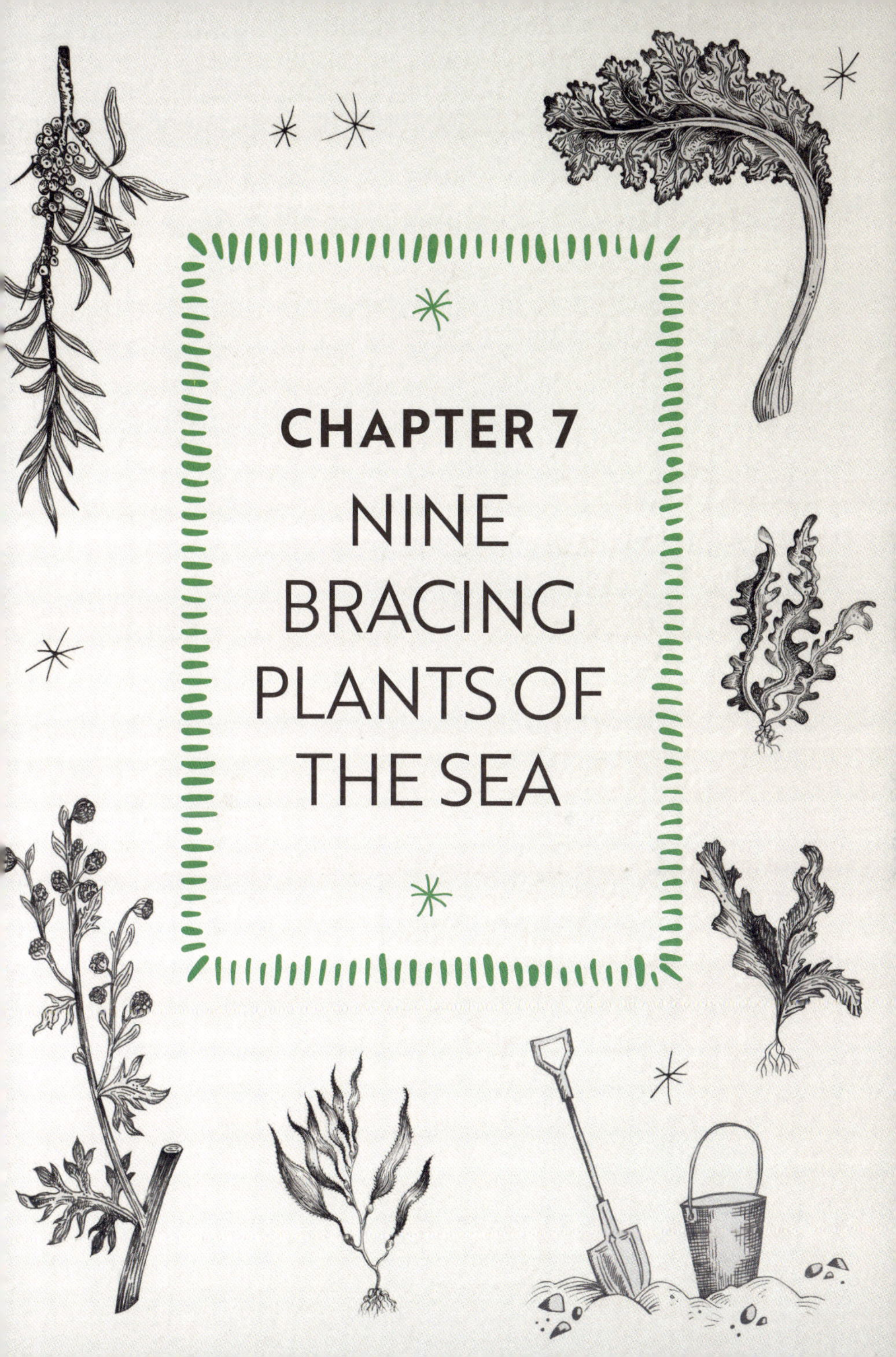

CHAPTER 7

NINE BRACING PLANTS OF THE SEA

Nine Bracing Plants of the Sea

If you have ever lived close to the sea, you're a lucky person. Even as I'm writing this, some 50km (30 miles) from the nearest beach, in my mind, nevertheless, I can hear the angry crashing and wailing of a stormy sea, and then the calm subsiding of more gentle waves, the hiccoughing sob of a child emerging from a tantrum, exhausted and needing to go to bed.

Once, I lived very close to the sea; so close that every year a man would come to scrape the salt from the windows. Me and my friends would go through the garden gate and down the steps to the water's edge, to the miles and miles and miles of waves, or we would run along the clifftops to see the tumbledown houses that had lost their battle with the elements, taken by the relentless incursion of nature. The shocking debris of the ruined homes was a stark reminder of just how vulnerable we humans are, for all our cleverness and ingenuity. Scattered spoons and forks, a dented kettle, smashed glass; it was a treasure trove for us kids, who ignored the laughable ropes that were meant to repel intruders. It's no wonder that even the most arrogant people are wary of the elemental forces that don't give a damn about us (and why should they?).

The cliffs are still eroding and the reason is because the land is a soft boulder clay; in some areas you can scratch it off with your fingernails. It was a wonderful place to be, especially if you love swimming in the North Sea, frigid in the summer and a killer in the winter. I'd go back in a heartbeat.

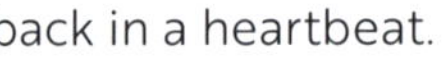

1. Beach wrack

(Fucus vesiculosus, Pelvetia canaliculata & Fucus serratus)

When a stormy sea has finished doing its damage, what remains is called beach wrack. This is a conglomeration of different kinds of seaweeds (and other "ingredients") that have been churned up and dumped on the shoreline by the receding waters. The names of the seaweeds are wonderful: bladderwrack (*Fucus vesiculosus*), channelled wrack (*Pelvetia canaliculata*) and serrated wrack (*Fucus serratus*). Many other kinds of wracks, as well as other seaweeds, sea grasses, dead marine plants and indeterminate bits of creatures, might end up caught up in beach wrack.

HOW TO IDENTIFY BEACH WRACK

Bladderwrack is an olive-brown colour, with branching fronds and air-filled "bladders" which, if left to go hard in the sun, can be popped like bubblewrap to the delight of children as well as adults. Channelled wrack, named for the "channels" that appear in the folded-in fronds, is the yellow-brown one that you often see on slipways and rocks, where care is needed not to slip and fall. Serrated wrack gets its name from the edges of its fronds, which look like the tines of a saw.

ALL ABOUT BEACH WRACK

Beach wrack is an important forageable resource, but possibly not in the way that you might expect (that is, edibility). Throughout the world and for many generations, people who lived close to the sea used beach wrack on the land, as a valuable fertilizer for crops. The gathering of this bounty was, at one time, a communal endeavour. In Ireland, the spring tide closest to Imbolc (St Brigid's Day, 1 February) was the most important of the year, everyone turning out to help gather the seaweed and shellfish.

Having said that, bladder wrack, channelled wrack and serrated wrack are all edible, if harvested when fresh and young rather than taken from fly-ridden, rotting heaps on the beach. They are a good source of omega fatty acids and iodine, as well as other minerals and vitamins. Edible seaweeds were eaten, along with fish and potatoes, during the meatless period of Lent before the Easter festivities.

Those who live close to the sea are more aware of its dangers and, accordingly, there are many superstitions that attempt to keep people safe from its treacherous arms. Where there is sea, there is danger, and where there is danger, there is superstition, and where there is superstition, there is a call to the gods. One of the superstitions in Ireland, which spread with European settlers to the Americas, was the belief that seaweed should not be gathered on a Sunday, or any other holy day, out of respect for the elemental forces of the waves. There was another idea that nothing but weeds would thrive where the land had been spread with seaweed on a Sunday. On the Isle of Lewis, there was a yearly sacrifice to the Shony, the anglicized name for the water spirit called Seonaidh. People gathered at the church at night, then one of the party would wade out into the black water and call to the creature:

> *"Shony, I give you this cup of ale, hoping you will be so kind as to send us plenty of seaweed for enriching our ground next year."*

The cup was thrown into the sea, and then the party began. Hopefully, whoever it was who waded bravely (and possibly with more than a few ales inside them) into the sea was given a fluffy towel and a cup of hot cocoa afterwards.

Forager's Choice by Julia Horton-Mansfield

Here is a recipe from my wonderful foraging friend Julia Horton-Mansfield. She owns an innovative restaurant and shop called The Really Wild Emporium, all to do with food, soaps and skincare made mostly from ingredients foraged locally, in and around St Davids, the tiniest city in the UK.

Julia's Super-easy Sweet and Sour Bladderwrack Pickle

The following simple pickle recipe is so useful. I make litres of the pickle liquid in one go, so that I have it ready for whenever I want to use it. You can strain the spices out if you prefer to remove them, but it seems wasteful as the pickle improves with them left in, and I personally love the flavour and texture of the spices along with the seaweed. You can tinker with the variety of spices and the amounts to suit your taste.

You will need:
2 litres/70fl oz/8½ cups apple cider vinegar
1.2kg/2lb 11oz granulated sugar
10 tsp coriander seeds
3 tsp mace
5 handfuls of bladderwrack tips

1. To make the pickle, put the vinegar and sugar in a pan, add the spices and gently bring to a simmer. Check that the sugar has all dissolved.

2. Cut and collect fresh young bladderwrack tips, rinse with cold water and drain well, then add them to a sterilized jar.

3. Pour the hot pickling liquid into the jar to fully cover the bladderwrack. Add the lid, but do not seal shut. Leave for 2–3 hours to cool. Once it has fully cooled, close the lid to seal.

4. Seal the jars with vinegar-proof lids and store in the cool, but out of sunlight. Shake occasionally when you remember. Wait a few weeks before you eat it.

2. Edible Seaweeds

(Porphyra umbilicalis, Macrocystis pyrifera & Ulva lactua)

Did you know that all seaweeds that we can find at the intertidal zone (that is, the ones that can be reached on foot) are edible? In Japan, people have been eating seaweeds for ever. They are nutritious, delicious and easy to find at most places where there's a clean sea. For us foragers, seaweed can be a total delight.

Here, we will look at three common seaweeds: laver aka nori (*Porphyra umbilicalis*), kelp (*Macrocystis pyrifera*) and sea lettuce (*Ulva lactua*).

HOW TO IDENTIFY LAVER, KELP AND SEA LETTUCE

These seaweeds can all be found around the world. Laver resembles a crumpled pink-purple plastic bag. You may have seen it sold as nori seaweed, in dried sheets.

Kelp is one of the most common kinds of seaweed to harvest. This is the large, brown ribbon-like "thing" that grows on underwater rocks that you can reach easily when the tide is low. They don't have roots as such, but instead attach to rocks which do the job just as well. The stipe (the stem of a seaweed – the same name is used for mushrooms) holds the kelp up toward the sunlight as it needs the sun. There are even kelp "forests" that are protected in some places in the world.

Sea lettuce is distinctive for its green, green colour and large sheets resembling lettuce leaves, which are sometimes as long as 1m (3¼ft), anchored onto rocks.

SAFETY: **Whatever seaweed you try, make sure that you remove all sand and gritty parts before eating. Do be aware that thyroid issues might be contraindicated and that seaweed is not advised if you are breastfeeding, because of the high iodine content.**

ALL ABOUT SEAWEED

Seaweed used to be added to the fodder of horses, cattle and other animals. These days, it is used in many ways, including in papermaking, pharmaceuticals and even being added to beer to make sure a pint has a good frothy "head".

Seaweed also has a long-standing connection with the Fairy Folk. In Scotland, the kelpie or water horse was a supernatural being that looked just like a real horse, except that it was covered in seaweed and had a habit of luring unsuspecting people into the water to drown them. Over the water, in Brittany, the korrigans were fairy beings who were said to ride across the sea with the sole reason of annoying the fishermen.

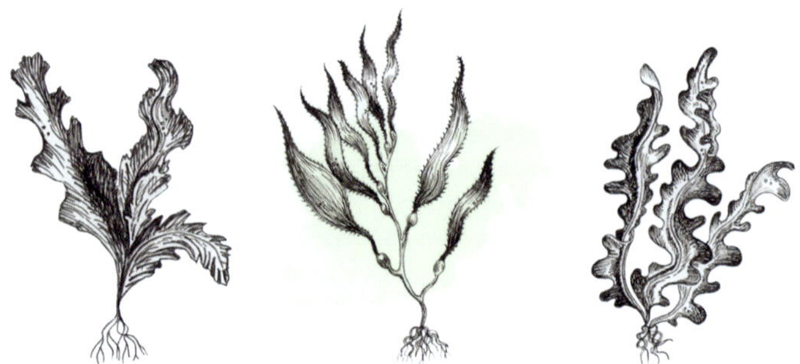

A friend of mine has a posy of seaweed on her porch, and she insists that this can tell the weather. If it shrivels, she tells me, it's going to be dry. I'm not certain if this is that useful because, after all, I could just as well look up at the sky.

While low in calories, seaweed is full of minerals, such as iodine, and the vitamins A, B, C and D. Try using kelp ribbons as lasagna sheets – a very healthy alternative to pasta. The translucent sheets of sea lettuce, when deep fried, make see-through "chips". Laver is used in laver bread, which is almost a national dish in Wales and traditionally paired with oatmeal and streaky bacon. Leave out the bacon for a veggie brunch, as in the next recipe.

Laver and Egg or Tofu on Toast

First, know that laver bread itself is not a bread but a purée of seaweed which needs to be boiled for several hours in a slow cooker. It can be bought, too, in tins if a simpler option is preferable (and that's the one used here).

To a 120g/4¼oz tin of laverbread, add 30g/1oz medium oatmeal and shape into little flat cakes approx 5cm/2in across and 1cm/½in thick. Fry the cakes in a little butter or oil for 2–3 minutes on each side. Eat with a fried egg or some fried flavoured tofu of choice.

3. Tree Mallow

(Malva arborea)

Whereas the marsh mallow, the one that was used to make the plumply sugary sweeties (*Althea officinalis*), is very rarely found in the wild these days, the tree mallow makes up for it, and does so in spades (and you might add in the buckets, too). Native to the coasts of western Europe and the Mediterranean, I have seen it for myself while on a Greek holiday and also, closer to home, on the westerly coast of Wales.

HOW TO IDENTIFY TREE MALLOW

To find this treasure, you need, preferably, to be close to the seaside. Although the plant sometimes grows in gardens, its proper place is within the scent of the ocean. At first sight, you might not even realize that it's a mallow, as it is an imposing creature, robust, some 3m (10ft) tall, with lovely purple or pink flowers and large leaves. These leaves are strong, made to excrete salts through special glands.

ALL ABOUT MALLOW

The fallen seeds of the tree mallow can survive quite happily, safe in an impermeable case that opens up when the time is right. This is the cause of some concern wherever the tree grows, as its ability to withstand a harsh climate along with its tough seeds means that some see the plant as invasive.

There is a notion that the earlier lighthouse keepers may have used mallow leaves as toilet paper.

What else could they do? (Incidentally, the poor lighthouse keepers were prone to hideous accidents in the course of their work, either falling from the lighthouse while mending the light or being sent mad by the deadly toxic mercury, which was used from the 1890s to help the light turn smoothly.)

Next time you see a mallow plant (of any kind), take a moment to stroke the leaves. Every part of the plant is soft, wonderful to the touch. The petals can be eaten as an addition to a salad, and if you find the seedhead, open it up to see a tiny little "wheel". This is called a mallow wheel or a mallow cheese, and is a satisfying, if small, snack. Mallow has a mucilaginous quality which means that its leaves and boiled roots can be used to thicken soups, broths and stews that need a little extra oomph.

Tree mallow is used in herbal medicine to treat sprains. The leaves are made into a poultice by cooking them in saltwater and applying them to the affected area. Pliny the Elder said that mallow was an aphrodisiac. He mentioned that when the seeds were sprinkled "for the treatment of women", they "stimulated sexual desire to an infinite degree".

4. Sea Holly

(Eryngium maritimum)

Called sea holly or sea eryngo, there's also a garden variety of this beautiful plant – beautiful, that is, if you admire plants that have spiny, fractal-looking leaves. Other names include flat sea holly, blue sea holly and, most lovely of all, sea star thistle. Old names include sea hulver or sea holm; "holm" refers to a flat place that is regularly submerged by floods. The plant is a member of the Apiaceae family, that is, the wild carrot family (which includes some very toxic members, as mentioned on pages 156–157). Sea holly is not poisonous, but please only forage the garden kind as it is becoming increasingly rare in the wild. It is illegal to dig up the roots. Look at and admire wild sea holly, but don't touch!

HOW TO IDENTIFY SEA HOLLY

In the wild this plant likes seaside areas such as shores, where there is plenty of sand and shingle and the soil is not liable to be acidic. It grows in stiff clumps, standing up straight and smart, up to some 90cm (3ft) tall (sometimes smaller in windy areas). The unusual spiky blue flowerheads are reminiscent of a thistle's, with a ruff of spiny bracts. The early leaves look a bit like sorrel leaves, but then become silvery blue, spiky and waxy. Sea holly loves to be out in the open sun; it refuses to hang around in the shade.

ALL ABOUT SEA HOLLY

Many of the plants associated with the sea are also associated with the Virgin Mary, who is called the Star of the Sea. Mary's blue colour is that of the sea and of the sea holly, too, and is also linked to the sky and to heaven. Plutarch, the philosopher and priest at the Temple of Apollo in Delphi, was rather less than lyrical in his observation of the plant, saying:

> *"They report of the sea holly, if one goat take it into her mouth, it causeth her to stand still, and afterwards the whole flock, until such a time as the shepherd takes it from her."*

Despite its spiky quality, sea holly was once used as a food source. The traditional use was to cook the young shoots and eat them in the same way as asparagus (dripping with lots of butter), while the roots were washed, dried and candied. In Shakespeare's time, sea holly had a reputation of being an aphrodisiac; at that time the candied sweets were called "kissing comfits". If you want to make sea holly sweets using the garden plant (not the endangered wild sea holly), you need to peel the roots and boil them like parsnips until tender, then peel and slice them and then boil the pieces again in a syrup of sugar and water. If you have the time to try this, please let me know how they taste.

The 16th-century herbalist John Gerard mentions their benefit to the reproductive organs too:

> *"If [. . .] preserved with sugar, they are exceedingly good to be given to old and aged people that are consumed [. . .] with age, and who want natural moisture'.*

Make of that what you will!

5. Gorse

(Ulex europaeus)

This plant is indigenous across western Europe, but, in common with many other plants, has made its home in other places too, from the Americas to the Antipodes. Other names include furze, whin and western gorse.

Although the emphasis here is on gorse as a plant of the seaside, it also loves to get to grips with mountainous areas, relishing the same harsh winds and other challenging weather conditions that affect coastal regions.

HOW TO IDENTIFY GORSE

This is a deciduous shrub, with small acidic-yellow, coconut-scented flowers, attaining some 1.5m (5ft) high and the same across. Gorse is in flower all the time, and similarly, the seeds ripen all year too, hence the proliferation of spiny prickles.

ALL ABOUT GORSE

This fast-growing plant is sometimes used as a living fence and a way of keeping animals corralled.

I knew that the coconutty scent was said to be beautiful but, try as I might, I just didn't "get" it. Then, during a trip to the sea on a hot sunny day, the scent of gorse as I opened the car door was incredible: a strongly fragrant aroma of bees and coconut and . . . something else that I had never noticed before, possibly a mix of it all, including the hot leather car seat, too. I realized that it was the heat that was needed for me to wallow in the deliciousness.

Gorse is one of the Bach flower remedies, to counter despair and hopelessness. There is something so uplifting about the jolly yellow flowers, which brighten up the depths of winter, that this makes sense. Some people use gorse flowers in tea to promote good digestion, or in a topical treatment for skin conditions such as eczema and acne.

For those of us that like to play with plant pigments, you will be happy to know that gorse flowers give a strikingly lovely bright yellow. Put your foraged flowers in a saucepan, cover with water and simmer for a couple of hours, then strain the liquid.

How to Pickle Gorse Buds

Gorse buds can be foraged all year round. Pickle them for use in salads in the same way as capers, and use the pickling vinegar in your vinaigrettes, too. Vintage storage jars are a nice touch.

1. Steep sun-warmed gorse buds in a vinegar of your choice (but not malt vinegar; think white wine vinegar or cider vinegar, for example).

2. Leave the gorse and vinegar for a few hours to turn yellow; this will happen most easily in a sunny spot.

3. Decant into clean, sterilized jars. Seal, label and store in a cool, dry place, and in the refrigerator once the jar is opened.

6. Sea Kale

(Crambe maritima)

You can find sea kale in northern France, Britain and other parts of Europe. The plant was brought to U.S. President Thomas Jefferson who planted it in his famed garden at his home Monticello around 1809. Also called crambe, this is similar to the "normal" kale that can be grown in a garden or bought in a store. So, why should I bring this alternative brassica to your attention?

Well, put simply, this chapter is about plants that you can gather from watery places, and we are foragers, and sea kale is free . . . And in the words (more or less) of the movie *Withnail and I*:

> *"We want the finest kale available to humanity, we want it here, and we want it now."*

(If you have never seen this movie, search it out immediately.)

HOW TO IDENTIFY SEA KALE

Sea kale grows to 60cm (24in) high, with generously large leaves and many small white flowers that, as with all cabbages, have four small petals (this is a good tip for identifying other plants in the same family). It can survive perfectly well in places where other plants would fear to tread, such as beaches of pebbles or shingles which have very little soil and are often drowned in rainwater mixed with water from the sea.

SAFETY: **Those with thyroid issues should seek medical advice if intending to eat plants of the cabbage family.**

ALL ABOUT SEA KALE

Sea kale is quite remarkable. It grows in the colder part of the year when nothing much else is around and was at first used for animal fodder as well as for us humans. It can withstand hot climates and cold, and, unlike "normal" kale, is tolerant of a higher level of salinity than other terrestrial plants, so it can grow in places where there are fewer competitors for what soil there is. It also doesn't care about which plants are pollinating it; for sea kale, anything goes!

Sea kale is high in vitamin C and is also a source of vitamin K as well as other vitamins and minerals. Along with all cruciferous veg, it is scientifically proven to help prevent colon cancer.

If you want to try sea kale for yourself, take leaves sparingly in case it's not for you. Scatter seeds along the upper shoreline to help future sea kale patches to grow.

7. Sea Spinach

(Beta vulgaris subsp. *maritima)*

Also called sea beet or wild spinach, this trusty seashore vegetable is one of the most common sea edibles, and also one of the easiest to find in coastal areas of Europe, northern Africa and southern Asia.

HOW TO IDENTIFY SEA SPINACH

The cousin to chard (*Beta vulgaris* subsp. *cicla*), sea spinach grows 60cm (2ft) high, and has matching green flowers. A giveaway for this seaside vegetable is the shiny succulent leaves; in older plants, the leaves are more crooked and a darker green. In summer, a flower spike may bear tiny green flowers. This plant likes to grow at the top end of pebble beaches, coastal cliffs and rocks, seemingly unaware of harsh climates. On occasion you might see it inland.

ALL ABOUT SEA SPINACH

The sweet-tasting root of sea spinach can be harvested and cooked, but it's better not to uproot an entire wild plant, so stick to the leaves. These leaves are another super-healthy delight for foragers, rich in vitamins and minerals. They can be treated as you would ordinary spinach, although it is more robust than that land-locked green. Choose the very young and tender leaves if you want to eat sea spinach leaves raw in a salad. Otherwise the leaves can be steamed or quickly wilted in the pan; or, if they are older, blanched in boiling water and stir-fried, the tough stems having been removed.

8. Sea Buckthorn

(Hippophae rhamnoides)

Sea buckthorn is found in coastal regions throughout Asia and Europe, and it is quite a beauty, with its sunshine orange berries and narrow silver-green leaves. The last time I went back home to Yorkshire, I managed to get to one of my favourite places in the world, Spurn Head, where I saw sea buckthorn for the first time. It's always exciting to find a plant that you've only seen before in photographs.

HOW TO IDENTIFY SEA BUCKTHORN

This is a large deciduous shrub, some 1.8m (6ft) tall, with narrow, silvery leaves and very thorny shoots. Tiny greenish-yellow flowers can be seen in racemes in the spring, followed by bright orange berries on the female plants.

ALL ABOUT SEA BUCKTHORN

Spurn Point is a nature reserve, a narrow and ever-changing spit, as little as 50m (164ft) wide in some places, that curves round the edge of the Humber estuary on one side, with the North Sea on the other. Along the spit the opposing forces of wind and wave battle relentlessly, as they have done for millennia, an argument that will never be resolved.

The last time I went to Spurn Point, I was impressed to see a shiny new visitor centre, but annoyed with myself that it had just closed for the day. However, the warden there chatted with me for a good half an hour, and he told me that the buckthorn, as there had been no grazing animals for years, was completely taking over. The solution was to clear away much of it and move Highland cattle into the area, using "Nofence" technology. Each cow is fitted with a GPS collar that is controlled by an app on a smartphone. If the cow meanders toward a virtual boundary, the animal hears a warning that increases in volume until it passes the boundary, whereupon it receives an electric pulse. The warden told me that the idea is working like clockwork, with cattle roaming over the desired area, eating up new shoots of sea buckthorn and other invasive species and leaving space for other plants to thrive.

Sea buckthorn berries have been hailed as a superfood because of their high level of vitamin C (five times more than oranges) and antioxidants as well as omega-3 and 6. The problem for us is that these marvellous berries are enclosed in ultra-sharp thorns. A foraging friend of mine (James of the Woodland Classroom) has perfected a way, though. Here is his tip!

Extracting Sea Buckthorn Juice

With a clean bucket and good gloves, squeeze along the buckthorn branch in a downward motion, toward the tip of the branch. This squashes the berries as you go, avoiding you getting spiked. The juice will run into the bucket. You will still need to separate the debris from the juice, though, and a sieve works well for this.

The best time to search for sea buckthorn berries is October and November. Bear in mind that anything that contains strong doses of vitamin C will be sour. Fruit leathers are a good option for using up your juice, but if you are not sure what to make or don't have the time just yet, pop it in the freezer for now.

9. Sea Mugwort

(Artemesia maritima)

Is this one a surprise? There are 180 different species of mugwort, so you're unlikely to be able to get to know all of them, but it is fun to try! The folk name for this plant is "old woman", a nod to the beautiful silver grey of the leaves. Very elegant indeed. Sea mugwort, also known as sea wormwood, is native to the Atlantic coasts of northern Europe, the UK, the Baltic States and more.

HOW TO IDENTIFY SEA MUGWORT

Unlike *Artemisia vulgaris*, this mugwort won't fare well in shade. Sea mugwort likes the drier areas of marshes, sand, shingle and suchlike. It grows to a height of 60cm (2ft), and produces spikes with small yellow-brown clusters of flowers. The leaves are feathery and aromatic.

SAFETY: **Although this plant has been used as a condiment, it can be poisonous if used in large quantities – even the aroma can result in a headache. While it has a number of medicinal uses, sea mugwort should be used only by a registered practitioner.**

ALL ABOUT SEA MUGWORT

See pages 14–16 for information about *Artemisia vulgaris*, which also applies to *Artemisia maritima*. However, as mentioned above, use sea mugwort only under the guidance of a professional medical herbalist

ALL ABOUT SOUTHERNWOOD

Let's consider southernwood (*Artemisia abrotanum*), another mugwort species of interest to foragers. It came from France originally but has spread its beauty far and wide. The leaves are soft, feathery and not as robust as other kinds of mugwort. When bruised, they give off a sweet lemon aroma, giving the plant its name citronelle, which means "lemon herb".

Another name for southernwood is garderobe, because it was used to repel various insects that might elsewise feast on peoples' clothes. Also, southernwood has long been used as a conditioner for people's hair, to make it shine and with the hopeful notion that it could make hair grow. Culpeper used the ashes of the leaves, mixed with oil, for the same reason. Otherwise, the plant was once upon a time used to protect wounds and speed the healing process. Its fragrance led it to be used as a strewing herb in the Elizabethan era.

CHAPTER 8

NINE CUNNING PLANTS THAT ARE FREE

Nine Cunning Plants That Are Free

It would be wrong to say that these plants are better than any other. But this chapter – "Nine Cunning Herbs That Are Free" – is a nod to some of the plants which, like those in the original spell and several others in the book, may go unnoticed because they are so common as to be unseen, and in some cases are not even looked for at all. We need to treasure these as fallen angels; they give us more than we know, and in some cases we have been reaping their benefits for hundreds (or thousands) of years. In some of these descriptions you may find echoes of the original nine plants of the spell. See what you spot as you turn these pages.

The funny thing that I have noticed is that the more you look at wild plants and trees and the like, and the more you use them and get to know them, the more your perception of what a "weed" is changes. No longer will so-called weeds be reviled. You will see them as friends, as allies, as unparalleled beings who should really be given the respect that they deserve.

Here's an idea! Who would like to have a day of worship, once a year, just for these plants? Let's do it!

1. Elder

(Sambucus nigra)

One of the plants that ought to be counted among the most magical (and an equal to any of the traditional nine) is the elder. If in any doubt, one of its prettiest folk names is fairy tree. Others include bore tree, deathwort, Devil's wood, God's stinking tree, hilder (meaning "hollow"), Judas tree, pipe tree and (just one more, folks) the catchy plant-of-the-blood-of-man. Elder was once so well respected that the branches were cut to enable easy access to the blossoms and berries, a little like coppicing.

HOW TO IDENTIFY ELDER

Elder is partly a shrub, partly a tree, and quite scruffy looking. At its highest, it reaches some 3.6–6m (12–20ft). In rural areas, it is chopped down in the summer months by huge, rattlingly cumbersome vehicles that bend shakily over the hedgerows, leaving the plant with a 1980s punk look. Elder can be found at the edges of wastelands, such as industrial estates and canal banks, verges and, notably, churchyards, where young saplings are left alone. This habitat is good for foragers, especially when the young shoots grow, the lacy white umbels of the flowers making way for the black berries a few months later. Its leaves include multiple oval leaflets with serrated edges, usually two or three pairs of leaflets with a single end leaflet.

SAFETY: **Elder contains cyanogenic glycosides, which are toxic. Cook or pickle the berries and flowers before consuming and don't eat any other part of the tree.**

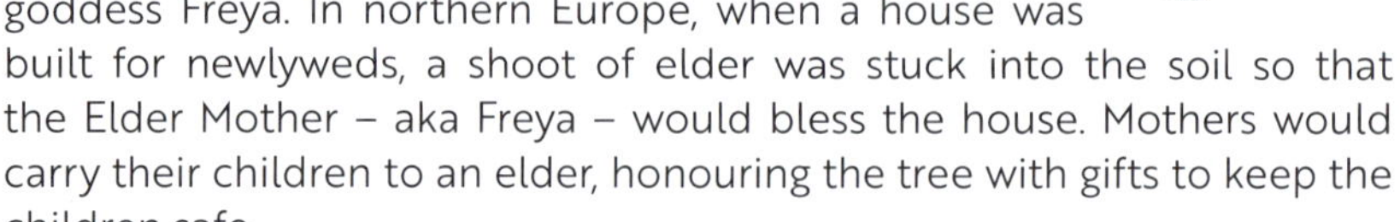

ALL ABOUT ELDER

The elder was a sacred tree in Norse mythology, dedicated to the thunder god Thor and to the fertility goddess Freya. In northern Europe, when a house was built for newlyweds, a shoot of elder was stuck into the soil so that the Elder Mother – aka Freya – would bless the house. Mothers would carry their children to an elder, honouring the tree with gifts to keep the children safe.

Elder was once believed to have been the tree on which Christ was crucified. Because of this idea, the tree was seen by some as evil in itself. Once upon a time, no self-respecting forester would cut it or use it. It was associated with death: a stick of elder was used to take the measurements of a coffin, and the driver of the hearse used a stick of elder as a whip.

It was also used to predict the weather. If an elder carried blossom and berry at the same time, a harsh winter was forecast. Other sayings tell us that "The weather never changes while the white elder is in bloom" and that "Elder bloom means eight weeks to harvest". In parts of mainland Europe, people would put elder twigs into water on 30 December. If all the buds flowered, there would be a good summer; if not, people would brace themselves for bad weather.

Usually in full flower around the time of the summer solstice, elder is also one of the many St John's herbs. This led to the elder being celebrated in fertility rites; one of the sayings was "On the feast of St John, elder blossoms make love even madder".

Elder is also a tree of protection. Branches were used to guard against fire and (optimistically) against lightning strikes. An elder stick would even keep werewolves at bay.

Elder is famed for its use in remedies for colds and flu. With this plant you can make two of the most wonderful healing concoctions: elderflower infusions in the spring/summer and elderberry elixir in the autumn.

Adele's Best Elderberry Elixir

You can buy bottles of elderberry over the counter if you wish . . . but as you look at the ingredients of any shop-bought remedy, you may think again. I have a better option for you. But you will need to wait until August, September or even November to make this recipe.

You will need:
25 umbels of foraged elderberries
A chunk of ginger, chopped
A few star anise
Burdock root
1 or 2 crab apples (or other apples) chopped
1 pear (if you have any), sliced
Sloes (if you have any ripe ones), just as they are
Stick of cardamom
A slug of apple cider vinegar (see page 34 for the recipe)
Honey, or even better jaggery sugar, to taste
A few cloves

1. One warm and sunny day, find yourself a pail, tub or large ziplock bag, then find some elderberries.

2. Don't rush, there's no hurry. Gather the berries diligently but respectfully, without pulling down branches or stripping them, for instance. You might think of this as a pilgrimage of sorts, a gathering of more than just the berries. As you gather, think of a world before cars, or mobile phones, or instant-access everything. Just try it. Know that with every moment, you're making something truly magical.

3. When home, remove leaves, stalks and debris.

4. When you're ready, add all the ingredients to the pan and cover with water. Bring slowly to the boil, remove from the heat and leave it, covered, overnight. Your house will smell like Hogwarts.

5. Strain and pour into clean, not previously used, plastic water bottles. Keep refrigerated, or freeze, leaving expansion room of a quarter of the elderberry liquid. (Glass bottles are more in keeping with the cottagecore look, but elixirs can be prone to explosions with temperature changes.)

6. Use as needed. Stir into porridge on winter mornings, for example, or use to make a warm drink. Every spoonful will remind you of the day you made the elixir. You will also find that you don't need as much sugar as you might think; taste before trying, and you may be surprised. It can also be frozen in those ziplock bags, used for the whole year until the next season of elder starts to arrive!

Forager's Choice by Sam Webster

Sam describes herself as a "feral neurospicy wildling who loves exploring and experimenting, learning new skills as I go along". She's foraged since she was a child, picking fruits with her nana and mum. She bought a book on mushrooms when she was 16 to copy the pictures for a GCSE art project and she still uses the book every autumn. In 2013 she was given a foraging course for her birthday and she hasn't been able to turn off that foraging instinct since. She's taught foraging since 2017 and she organizes the British Wild Food Festival. Soaking up every fact and flavour, she has made foraging her life, especially since taking part in the Wildbiome Project in 2025 when she experienced living solely off wild foods.

Sam's Elderflower Marmalade

Makes a 300ml/10½fl oz jar.

You will need:
2 oranges, chopped into short matchsticks
3 lemons, chopped as above
10 elderflower heads, stems removed and chopped as above
(Or use lemons, oranges and elderflowers left over from cordial making)
2kg/4lb 8oz sugar

1. Put the fruit and flowers in a large pan or jam pan and add 2l/70fl oz/8½ cups water.

2. Boil until the citrus fruit are cooked and the liquid is reduced by about half.

3. Add the sugar and heat until the sugar is dissolved, then boil, as for any other jam, until the setting point is reached (you can tell the setting point has been reached using a thermometer or the more traditional method of placing a small blob of the jam onto a cold plate from the freezer and pushing the blob with your finger . . . the jam is ready when the blob wrinkles).

4. Store in clean, sterilized jars and enjoy.

Sam's Elderflower Marmalade Cake

You will need:

125g/4½oz butter, at room temperature, plus extra for greasing
2 large eggs
3 heaped tbsp elderflower marmalade
250g/9oz self-raising flour
1 tsp baking powder
4 tbsp icing/powdered sugar

1. Preheat the oven to 190°C/170°C fan/375°F/gas mark 5. Grease and line a 20cm/8in circular cake pan.

2. Put the butter, eggs, 2 heaped tablespoons of the marmalade, and the flour and baking powder in a food processor or large mixing bowl.

3. Beat together well, but don't overdo it – about 15 seconds in the processor. Scrape the mixture down and mix again for 5 more seconds in the processor.

4. Tip into the tin and cook for 45–60 minutes. Test after 45 minutes with a toothpick. When it comes out clean, the cake is done.

5. Take the cake out of the oven and leave in the pan for 10 minutes before turning out onto a wire rack to cool. You can leave the liner on until the cake is served.

6. Once the cake is cool, mix a teaspoon of marmalade with the icing sugar and a little water and drizzle over the top. Store in an airtight box.

2. Daisies

(Bellis perennis & Leucanthemum vulgare)

Here, we are looking at two different daisies: the smaller one, aka *Bellis perennis*, and the oxeye daisy, *Leucanthemum vulgare*. Both plants are part of the huge family Asteraceae, also called the sunflower family. This is one of the largest of all plant families, with some 25,000 species (that we know about) scattered around the globe. If you know chicory, feverfew, safflower, lettuce, dandelion, artichoke and artemisia, then you probably know more about Asteraceae than you first thought.

The common daisy has an impressive number of folk names for such a small flower: bachelor's buttons, dog daisy, cat-posy, Margaret's herb, bairnwort, garden daisy, jackanapes, silver penny, maudlinwort and many more. Some of these speak for themselves, others are a mystery to be revealed (or not).

HOW TO IDENTIFY DAISIES

These daisies have similarities that can cause confusion. It's not unusual for newby foragers to think that they are the same plant, the small daisy grown larger. This is not the case!

The common or garden daisy (*Bellis perennis*) is recognizable from its yellow head of many tiny flowers surrounded by white petals, however it also comes in other colourways, including with pink, red or white flowers.

Oxeye daisies are much taller (up to 60cm/24in), with larger flowers; the sight of these flowers blowing in the wind is the epitome of summer. The leaves look similar to those of the chrysanthemum; no surprise that they, too, are part of the Asteraceae tribe.

ALL ABOUT THE COMMON DAISY

There's one particularly lovely trait of this flower. At night, or when the rain falls, the daisy "goes to sleep", the petals opening again when the sun comes out (the oxeye daisy does not close in this way). Not everyone is aware of this, as I know from taking so many foraging walks. Daisy's wide-open flower is

designed for pollinators to feast from, which might be a reason to leave them alone in the summer.

There are several stories of how the common daisy got its name. In one, a tree nymph called Belides was fleeing Vertumnus, god of spring and orchards; to escape him she changed herself into the flower. Another version sees Flora, goddess of the flowers, chased by Boreas, god of the north wind; to impress her, Boreas blew a snowy wind over her flowers. This didn't faze Flora; she simply turned the snowflakes into daisies.

One of the common daisy's name folk names is bairnwort. Bairn is a Scottish word for a child, from the Old Norse. Children love daisies, which might be part of the reason for the name, or it might also be because the daisy flower is used to alleviate bruises, likely to affect active children, who like climbing trees and jumping off walls, etc.

Daisy is a symbol of innocence, youth and virtue. Famously, it is used as a divinatory tool. As the person holds the flower they pull off the petals one by one, calling out "He loves me . . . he loves me not . . ." until the last petal is reached and the verdict is set.

A magical remedy for fevers of all kinds worked like this: The patient would eat nine daisies; three on day one, then two more on each subsequent day until a total of nine had been reached. Then, the number was reduced backward in the same way, until one was back to eating the last three. If the fever didn't abate, the remedy was repeated. An interesting idea, and if anyone wants to try it, please do let me know the outcome.

ALL ABOUT THE OXEYE DAISY

All parts of the plant are edible; the leaves are particularly good either as a foraging nibble or in a mixed salad, to add some glamour to a summer meal. The yellow part is even nicer, but before you get stuck in, shake to dislodge any critters that might be in the middle of their dinner, too!

It was considered bad luck to step on the first oxeye of the year. Bouquets of the flowers needed to be picked with your eyes closed; the number of flowers gathered would equal the years of your marriage. How on earth it would be possible to gather flowers with your eyes shut, I have no idea.

The oxeye has been used as medicine for whooping cough. Otherwise, it is believed to be antispasmodic and a diuretic.

Daisy Remedy (for Bruises)

One of the folk names for the garden daisy is bruisewort. This is a simple recipe for a soothing balm that works in the same way as arnica (*Arnica montana*), without expense.

You will need:

Daisies (flowers and stems)
Oil (olive or vegetable)
Beeswax
Small clean, sterilized jars with a lid, such as a small jam jar
A week of sunny days

1. Pick the daisies on a sunny day (so they are dry) and gently squash them to fill the jar halfway.

2. Cover with the oil, removing any air pockets.

3. Put the lid on and leave it in a sunny window for a week, shaking each day.

4. After a week, strain the oil, place with the beeswax in a heatproof bowl over a saucepan of boiling water and gently heat, stirring until the wax melts and you have a smooth balm.

5. Pour the balm into a clean, sterilized jar (with a lid) and leave to set in the fridge until needed.

3. Jack-by-the-Hedge

(Alliaria petiolata)

Other names for this commonly ignored "weed" include hedge garlic, mustardweed, poor man's mustard, hedge penny and sauce weed. This is a member of the cruciferous family; crucifer means "cross-bearing" and refers to the shape of the four-petalled flowers. The family is also called Brassicaceae and it includes over 3,000 species around the globe.

As I am writing these very words, it is winter. Despite the bitter cold, a dog needs to go for a walk, and it's also a good way to start a day for me, too. I wasn't thinking about much but as we walked along briskly, I realized that there were young leaves of this herb cluttering the verges, raring to grow, so I gathered a few to see what they were like. Back home, washed and drained, the leaves were flavoursome and tasty, so I popped them into a pan to make a wholesome thick soupy stew for lunch.

HOW TO IDENTIFY JACK-BY-THE-HEDGE

It took me a while to find this plant, simply because it didn't grow where I lived at the time. This is where the foraging books come in. If you continually look at them then, one day, you will find Jack-by-the-hedge, and you will meet it with delight as a friend that you know well (even if you hate the flavour). I found it is a herb of hedges and overlooked banks, where it likes to live in the shade. It grows from 30cm (12in) to as high as 1.2m (4ft), with heart-shaped leaves that smell garlicky when crushed. Its small white flowers grow in clusters at the end of the stems.

(A good way to identify many plants of the cabbage family is the four-petalled flowers, whether white, yellow or even pink/lilac.)

SAFETY: Those with thyroid issues should seek medical advice if intending to eat plants of the cabbage family.

ALL ABOUT JACK-BY-THE-HEDGE

Jack-by-the-hedge, aptly known as garlic mustard, is not to everyone's taste; it's a love/hate thing. If you can't tolerate wasabi, then you might want to leave it alone. If, however, you like such flavours, you will find this a delicious and even (dare I say) exotic vegetable, malingering in a hedge, waiting for someone to admire its startling surprise.

Crush the leaves to inhale a delicate garlic aroma, which has been used for centuries as a flavouring for fish and lamb or in a lovely spring salad; the pretty white petals and flowerheads are a mix of sweet and hot. Last time I was in Borough Market in London, Jack-by-the-hedge was being sold alongside wild sorrel – the price of both these weeds would make you cough!

Like cabbages of all kinds, Jack-by-the-hedge contains vitamins K, B6 and C.

A Tasty Side Dish

This is another very simple yet delicious recipe.

Steam a generous fistful, per person, of Jack-by-the-hedge, washed and patted dry. If also steaming any other cabbages, kale, etc, leave the Jack-by-the-hedge until last. Finish with soy sauce or a smidgen of shaved horseradish.

4. Cuckoo Flower

(Cardamine pratensis)

Other folk names include lady's smock, mayflower, fairy flower and milkmaids. The name cuckoo flower is also used by other plants, such as wood anemone or bluebell.

HOW TO IDENTIFY CUCKOO FLOWER

This often-over looked little flower appears in damper places, such as roadside ditches, riverbanks and, I have noticed, in uncut grassland too. A stalk of up to 60cm (24in) grows from a rosette of leaves (made up of pairs of oval leaflets) and bears racemes of delicate flowers with the characteristic cruciform four petals. Flowers come in shades of white, pink, even lilac.

SAFETY: **Those with thyroid issues should seek medical advice if intending to eat plants of the cabbage family.**

ALL ABOUT CUCKOO FLOWER

The flower is among many others that are reckoned to "wake" when the cuckoo is first heard in the spring. According to the British Trust for Ornithology, cuckoos are no longer seen as much as they used to be.

This pretty little plant looks innocent; but if you bite any of it – flower, leaf or even stem – you will be astonished at the fiery taste. As for medicinal uses, these include for skin conditions, asthma and as a diuretic and appetite stimulant. I have eaten enough of it while coaxing people to try it, and it does make you feel hungry!

Forager's Choice by Rob Gould

Rob grew up in the Cotswolds with an avid interest in nature and the outdoors and a love of good food. As a result of this combination, he has now been a forager for over half his lifetime, and teaching for more than half a dozen years. During that time, he says, he has been fortunate to work with wonderful chefs, cookery schools and mixologists, and this has led to him being able to hone his own ideas around food creativity.

Nowadays Rob spends most of his time teaching foraging on public and private walks, working at various festivals including the British Wild Food Festival, leading events with large corporate groups, consulting with restaurants and bars, and running workshops on the principles of fermenting and preserving. He has become very interested in promoting ethical meat eating, and to that end he teaches wild game butchery with his great friend Alex McAllister-Lunt.

Rob's Fermented Wild Mustard

I love to have a pot or two of this set aside each autumn to pep up dishes or to use sparingly as a condiment – sparingly as it's often only possible to make small amounts with the seeds you manage to gather.

Over the course of late summer into autumn, collect as many seeds as you can from wild mustard (*Sinapis arvensis*) or other members of the family – I often bulk out wild mustard seeds with seeds of Jack-by-the-hedge.

You will need:
Dried or fresh mustard seeds as well as other flavour bombs, wild or cultivated. This is a guide, not a precise recipe, so balance the flavours to your taste . . . at least ¾ of the blend should be mustard seeds. I like including a selection of the following:

- Wild garlic seeds, or a few fresh leaves
- Dried seaweed (even better dried over a smoky campfire)
- Hogweed seeds, dried or fresh (or toasted)
- Alexander seeds
- Horseradish root (if you can't get permission to dig some, buy it)
- Bay leaves
- Chillies (homegrown if possible)

1 teaspoon runny honey
Good-quality vinegar, ideally live (with the "Mother"; I use homemade beer or cider vinegar, but shop-bought is absolutely fine)
Salt

1. Get a clean jar that's about four times the volume of your gathered mustard seeds and weigh it. Make a note of that weight. I like to use a clip-top jar with a rubber gasket, but use what you have to hand.

2. Next, put a small glug of honey in the bottom of the jar. Barely a teaspoon or so.

3. Add the other flavourful ingredients you're using and then the mustard seeds – putting them on top helps to hold the other ingredients down.

4. Now pour in just enough vinegar to cover all your ingredients. If they start floating off the bottom, stop adding vinegar.

5. The second-to-last ingredient is water. You want about the same volume of water in the jar as seeds.

6. Now weigh the jar and subtract the initial weight to give you the weight of what's inside it. Note that down.

7. Our last ingredient is salt. We want 3 per cent salt to the weight of the contents of the jar. So divide your total ingredient weight noted above by 100, then just multiply it by 3. Sprinkle that quantity of salt on top of everything else, and pop your lid on loosely – as the ingredients ferment, you're going to get carbon dioxide and you don't want your jar turning into a bomb!

8. I tend to leave my wild mustard to ferment for a couple of months on the kitchen counter, but a fortnight or so should be fine. Drain off, retaining the liquid brine. Blitz the seeds in a mixer, or a pestle and mortar, to the required consistency, adding some of the brine back in if necessary. Put in a more conveniently sized clean, sterilized jar, and leave for a few days in the fridge for the flavour to blend through and mellow out. Store the mustard in the fridge.

5. Chickweed

(Stellaria media)

This is yet another very common plant that people simply don't see. The name chickweed tells you something, at least. It is eaten by chickens (and chicks).

HOW TO IDENTIFY CHICKWEED

It is often seen underneath the canopy of a tree, in the shade, in damp soil. If you happen to see it in such an environment (generally in the spring and summer), get closer and have a look. The plant forms a mat of tangled stems with oval leaves growing between 5cm (2in) and 35cm (14in) high; the stems themselves can be identified by a distinctive single line of hairs. The tiny, white, star-like flowers, with five two-lobed petals, are breathtakingly pretty.

ALL ABOUT CHICKWEED

The flowers and tender leaves are tasty. I recall one kid of six years or so who wolfed down a surprising amount of chickweed; sometimes children prefer to eat veg they have found themselves, and as long as they know only to eat what they've been told is safe, this is an ideal scenario! Chickweed is at its best when cleaned properly and used raw, and it is surprisingly filling. It is high in vitamin C; sailors, it is said, soaked the herb in vinegar as a way of alleviating scurvy.

Apparently, a sprig of chickweed was carried deliberately as a message of attraction. There's also a notion that, to make sure your loved one remained faithful, you should feed them chickweed.

6. Herb Robert

(Geranium robertianum)

What's the connection between Herb Robert, the robin and a Shakespearean character? See page 198 for the answer!

Herb Robert is one of those plants that, if noticed at all, tends to end up in the compost bin as an unnecessary weed, even for the best of gardeners. But look closer and you'll see a captivating little plant, a member of the cranesbill or geranium family. Known as Robert's geranium in the USA, it has one of those love/hate scents that some find repulsive and others delight in.

HOW TO IDENTIFY HERB ROBERT

In common with most geraniums, herb Robert, when crushed between thumb and forefinger, releases a scent that's strong enough for people to catch at some 90cm (3ft) away (and yes, I did test this!). The bright red colour of the stem, the delicately lacy leaves and the pert flower, with its pinky colour, along with the beak-like seedheads, really do deserve a closer look. Once you get to know it you will see it everywhere; in woods, along hedges, as an illegal squatter in tidy gardens, and tucked away unnoticed in wastelands. This is a shame, though. With a little imagination and no budget whatsoever, a gardening volunteer at Talgarth Mill (a working mill not far from where I live) dug up all the random herb Roberts and repatriated them all in one large space. It looks spectacularly wonderful, so charmingly great that inquisitive visitors to the mill's gardens often can't work out what the plant actually is.

ALL ABOUT HERB ROBERT

The name is herb Robert, but it's likely to be in honour of St Rupert, a 7th-century Austrian bishop. Then again, it seems that there were other bishops of the same, or similar, name. Once upon a time, its name was the rather grandiose *herba sanctii ruperti*. Forager's tip: if you use this rather high fallutin' name, people always look at the plant more carefully, impressed by the sound of it.

That interesting "mousy" smell, when crushed, might not be to everyone's taste, but the juice can be used as an insect repellent. If you are someone who suffers from bites, rub your skin with the leaves and, hopefully, there should be no more problems.

According to the Doctrine of Signatures, the look of a plant tells us what use it has for us – and so the red colour of the stems and other parts means that herb Robert is a tonic for the blood. (Sometimes this works, but it might just be a case of good luck.) A better way to use the plant is for its astringent qualities, as an infusion used as a gargle for a sore throat. It can also be used for cuts and bruises, even as an eyebath for conjunctivitis.

And the question about the name? Herb Robert is also called red robin, which, it is whispered, might be in honour of Robin Goodfellow, an interesting person of the folkloric realm who is said, because of his job as an occasional house elf, to be in need of a decent shower.

In Germany, he is called Knecht Ruprecht, and as Puck he has a cameo in Shakespeare's *A Midsummer Night's Dream*.

7. Fat Hen

(Chenopodium album)

This is another useful plant, mainly unseen or disregarded, but nevertheless one to watch out for. Other names include lambs' quarters, white goosefoot, pigweed, good King Henry, even muckweed.

A few years ago, I was delighted to get an email from Cardiff University. They were interested in finding out more about wild foods, and the culmination of the project was to work out what had been eaten by prehistoric people in the UK, and which foods were still being used after thousands of years. The end result was to be a banquet of sorts that, hopefully, would at least be edible.

We tend not to think very much about where our food comes from these days; we have so much abundance of just about everything. So this was an unusual and interesting task. The only restriction was that the food had to be plant based and/or animal friendly. Seven ingredients made the cut: crab apples, oats, hazelnuts, milk (originally auroch), elderberries, blackberries, barley . . . and fat hen.

HOW TO IDENTIFY FAT HEN

Fat hen grows 1–2m (3¼–6½ft) tall, with matt, grey-green leaves that are diamond in shape, like a goose's foot (hence the name). Fine white hairs give the leaves and stems a fuzzy appearance, and green-white flowers grow on spikes. Fat hen especially likes disturbed soil, such as wastelands, fields and gardens.

ALL ABOUT FAT HEN

Fat hen was, once upon a time, a trusted dietary staple, and it has never really gone away. It was there during the time of Tollund Man, whose 2,000-year-old body was found in Jutland, Denmark, in 1950. His story is unclear, but it is known that he was hanged, maybe as a sacrifice, and thrown into the bog where his remains were pickled by the acidic peat. Among the ingredients of his final meal were barley, linseed and fat hen.

I suspect that the very abundance of fat hen might be why it is so often overlooked; literally as "common as muck", hence the derogatory name of muckweed. In the farming area close to where I live, the crop that remains after the harvest is acres and acres of fat hen. Although it is nutritious and tasty, with a filling, mealy flavour, no one wants it because of that very abundance. In very little time, the thousands of seeds that fall into the fertile soil will lead to more plants appearing, and then yet more seeds falling.

Good King Henry is another branch of the goosefoots; its name is the grand-sounding *Chenopodium bonus-henricus*. It is similarly hardly noticed, although the leaves are somewhat more stately, sometimes with a red tint. Good King Henry is a character rather like the legendary Robin Goodfellow, who we have just met (see page 198).

8. Hawthorn

(Crataegus monogyna)

If ever there was a plant that belonged to the fairies, this is the one. Hawthorn is at its beautiful best in May, hence the old name of May blossom or maythorn. Other names include quickset, whitethorn, haw and mealy tree, this last a nod to the "mealy" texture of the raw young leaves that children used to like to eat as they walked to school. If you think that this is quaint, let me tell you about a woman that I know, now in her 80s, hale and hearty, only just retired from many years' public service, and living in the same area for all her life.

She told me that, yes, people really did nibble on hawthorn. But I was amazed that she also added how poor they were then; she and her sister had to share one pair of shoes between them on the way to school. Her story really shocked me, a reminder of how fortunate many of us are, just like me (and maybe like you) taking so much for granted. If you are a fairly seasoned forager, you will know hawthorn. However, whereas most people know about it, not everyone knows what it looks like.

HOW TO IDENTIFY HAWTHORN

Often seen in hedges, hawthorn is a shrubby plant or a small thorny tree, depending on how you look at it. The thorns can be quite vicious, so beware; a large and sprawling hawthorn can catch you unawares, even requiring scissors to free long hair.

I would love for you to be able to go out right now and have a look at a hawthorn tree in blossom. You might have never really seen the tree at all before. If you are able to do this, please give it some time to really

SEE the tree. When you do, it's almost as though you have a different sense coming into use. The flowers are very pretty, white or pinkish, with five petals and pink-purple anthers. The leaves are unusual, with five lobes; and then there are the thorny stems already warned against.

ALL ABOUT HAWTHORN

This is one of the magical plants that some believed should not be allowed into a house lest the fairies get in there and cause havoc. This tree has been regarded as one with special powers; therefore, it needs to be approached with care, not only in the practical sense (see long-hair hazard). One of the many special traits of the hawthorn is that it was said to be born from a bolt of lightning, hence its use in funeral pyres a long time ago. The power of its fire helped the deceased person to get to heaven. The tree was used in Greece and Rome in wedding rituals too; as recently as 1897 hawthorn flowers were still being used for bridal wreaths. Hopefully the bride wore gloves.

In earlier times, the hawthorn symbolized the renewal of nature – the tree was a symbol of hope. It would be nice to keep this alive, along with the idea of the maypole. Hawthorn was also used in banishing evil spirits, which means that it was effectively an exorcist. You might also want to see if hawthorn brings you good luck; all you need is to find a stick and pop it somewhere in your house, where it will do its lucky thing. This sounds too easy.

As with many plants, pagan ideas about hawthorns were translated into Christian ones. Some of them became "mass trees", dedicated to saints of the new religion. One of the most famous such trees appears in the story of Joseph of Arimathea. He was sent to Britain by an apostle and founded the first church in Glastonbury, at Wearyall Hill. A hawthorn grew from Joseph's staff and is said to have blossomed every year. The original tree is long gone, but a memorial stone marks the spot where it grew.

In herbal medicine, the hawthorn is used as a heart tonic. It improves blood circulation and is used for circulatory issues. Chinese herbalism has been using hawthorn for over a thousand years; one of the original names of the medicine means "to open the network of the heart".

Hawthorn Fruit Leather

You will need:

A large amount of ripe, washed hawthorn berries

Half the volume of good apple juice

1. Simmer the berries in the juice for 20 minutes, then let cool.

2. Mash the berries through a fine-meshed sieve. Spread the pulp thinly (3mm/⅛in) on a baking sheet lined with baking parchment.

3. Dry on a very low heat in the oven, or in a dehydrator if you have one, until the "leather" is . . . leathery.

4. When cold, cut into long strips and roll up, or else cut out stars or other shapes. The leathers should store for 3 weeks in a sealed container, but they are unlikely to last this long.

9. Yarrow

(Achillea millefolium)

This plant, more than most others, was a huge part of my own healing process, for reasons that I will explain later. In the meantime, know that this unassuming plant is mighty, despite its seeming humility. Folk names are plentiful, including old man's pepper, thousand weed, bloodwort, carpenters' weed, woundwort, Devil's nettle, staunchweed and many more including herb militaris, as the plant was used to staunch the flow of blood. Yarrow comes from the Old English name *gearwe*, pronounced as "yerw".

HOW TO IDENTIFY YARROW

Yarrow is a part of the Asteraceae family and can be identified by its clusters of tiny daisy-like flowerheads, with a yellow centre surrounded by off-white petals, sometimes with a lilac-ish colour. It grows to about 1m (3¼ft) tall, with feathery leaves. If you give the leaves or flowers a good squeeze, depending on your sense of smell, you might find that the aroma is quite pungently medicinal, reminiscent of chrysanthemums. It grows in a variety of grassy places.

ALL ABOUT YARROW

Yarrow has been used since time immemorial as a styptic, to heal wounds, including staunching the annoyance of a shaving cut. The plant is also good for nosebleeds. In the Middle Ages, prior to the arrival of hops in parts of Europe, yarrow was used along with other herbs (including mugwort, see pages 14–16, heather and others) to flavour beer. It is still used as an ingredient in some digestive bitters.

The first botanical name of this versatile plant – *Achillea* – has a breathtaking story to tell; as you would imagine in a plant of such heroic stature, accounts differ. In one, the Greek superhero Achilles was taught about plants by the centaur Chiron and so was able to use yarrow for his soldiers' injuries. However, when

Achilles was a baby, his mother dipped him into the magical river Styx to ensure that he would be protected everywhere the water touched. As she held him by the heel, this part was missed, so the hero succumbed to a fatal wound on his heel during the Trojan wars. *Millefolium*, or "thousand leaves", refers to yarrow's mass of leaves.

Yarrow is used in a divinatory practice described in the *I Ching* ("Book of Changes"). If you want to try it, you will need 50 yarrow stalks (although there is also a method that calls for coins instead), which are used in a complex process to generate hexagrams that are then interpreted. We don't know exactly why yarrow stalks were used; perhaps it was because of their long, straight sticks. The Druids also used yarrow as a divinatory tool to work out what the weather might do.

I love yarrow; so often ignored, especially in the winter months when only the stalks are left in the long grass. And here's my own story to add to the lore of this intriguing plant. When I had cancer, I found, with each session of chemotherapy, that it was getting more and more difficult to eat. I can't tell you how horrible this was. I needed to eat to allow the drugs to do their work, but although I was starving, it was impossible to get food to where it needed to be for more than a few minutes.

Then I had a call from Barbara, a friend who is a stalwart of the Herb Society. She sent me a new paper on yarrow which noted that the plant could be taken as a tea to help people keep food down. This was a new finding, and I was incredibly lucky that Barbara had read the paper. The dried yarrow did the trick within a few days. It was like a miracle

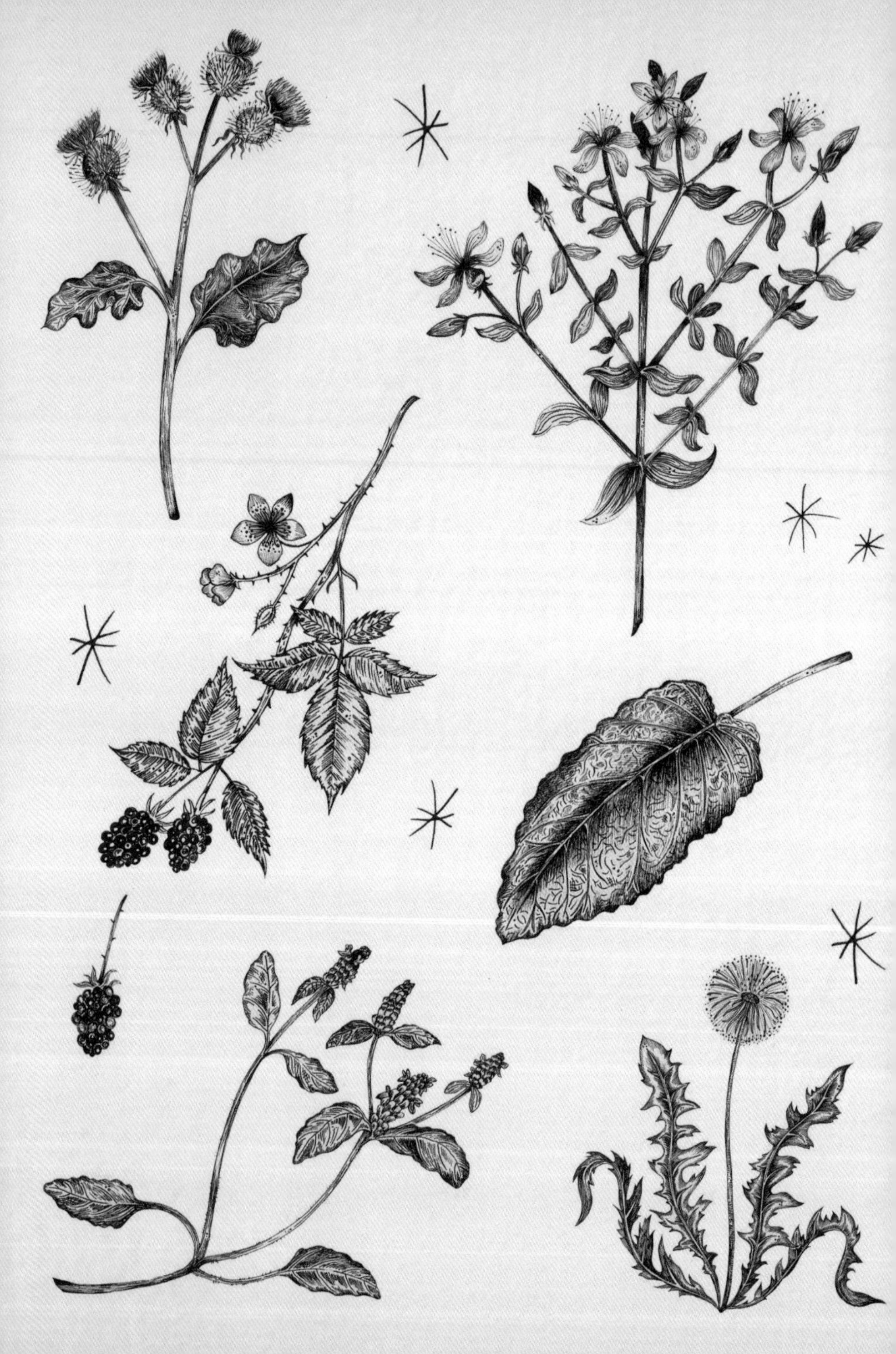

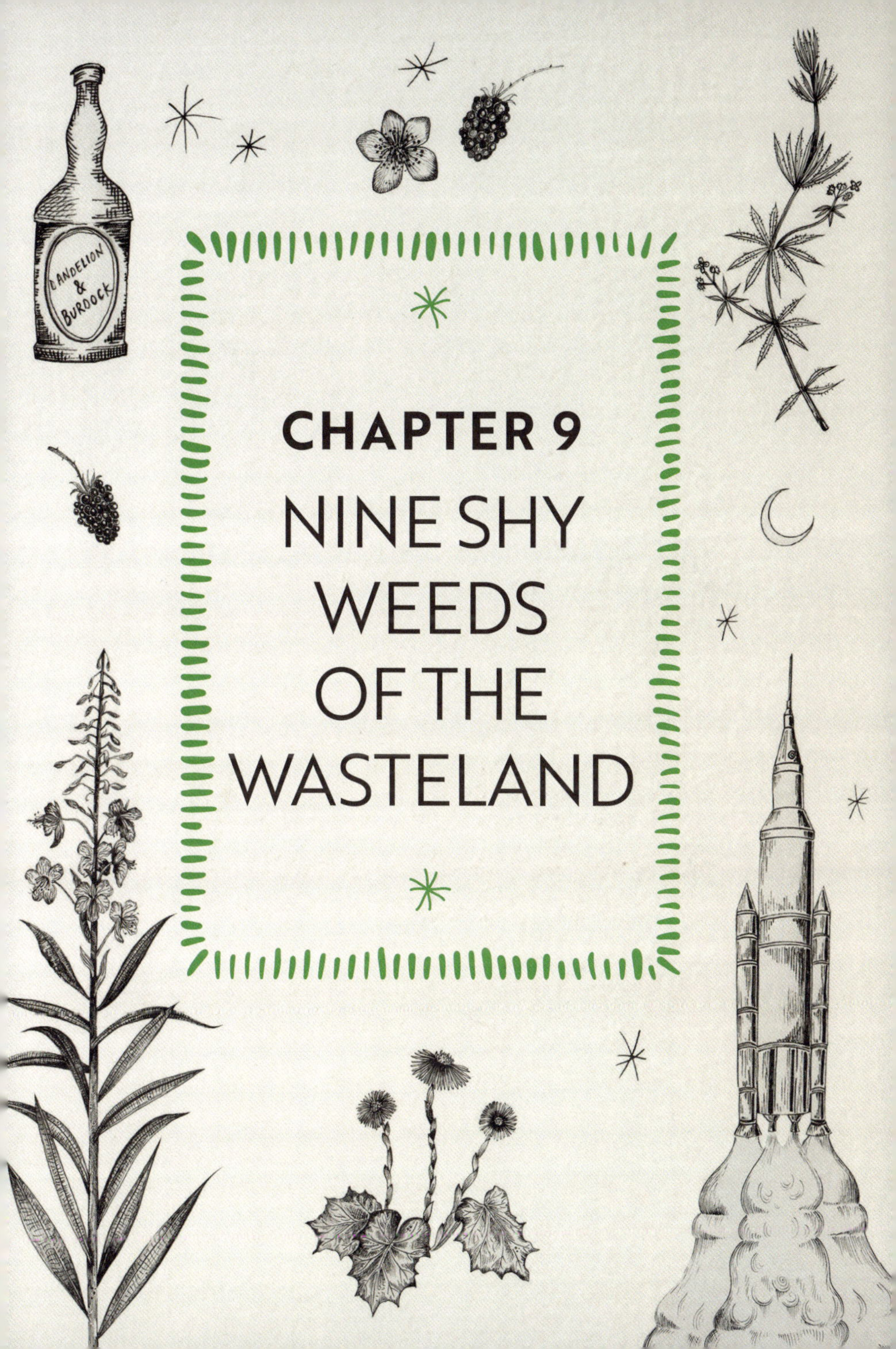

CHAPTER 9

NINE SHY WEEDS OF THE WASTELAND

Nine Shy Weeds of the Wastelands

Today, my border collie dog, Liz, doesn't want to go for a walk. She doesn't want any breakfast, either. Nor will she be seen by anyone at all for the rest of the day, apart from me. Liz is curled underneath the desk I'm sitting at, a quivering ball of fur, with the occasional nudge from me so she knows I'm here.

The reason for her anxiety is a looming geopolitical conflict (and it affects her body in the same way as loud fireworks). The why and wherefore of this particular conflict really doesn't matter, but this involves all of us. No matter which argument, which misunderstanding, which power-hungry sociopath it is this time; which megalomaniac lunatic it is who wants to inscribe himself into the very firmament; which presidents and ministers are acting only in their own interests; and all of this out of our hands as though democracy has been disregarded.

All this, right now, is resulting in infantry mortars just a few miles away from an otherwise calm and happy place, the repeated "cromp! cromp!" of weapons built by us all in order to kill us all too . . .

All this results in a little dog that hates conflict of any kind quaking every few minutes before an unknown evil.

If this is how a little dog can feel, think of the impact on people, on all those in the world who have no choice but to escape from their homes for the sake of their children and families. When we see news reports on the TV or social media, there's a disconnect; we are a million steps away from reality. I'm guilty of this, too. I don't have any answers, except to focus on what is good in the world.

The next stories are about resilience, a quality that we all need these days and that is shared by these important plants which we dismissively term "weeds". As with the original nine plants, they are all incredibly easy to find and are as comfortable as a stroll in the park, and for that normality, are undervalued and reviled.

1. Dandelion

(Taraxacum officinale)

Dandelions are *old*. Believed to have evolved some 30 million years ago, they belong to the Asteraeceae, and it's likely that we don't know just how many different species of dandelion there are. If you are a regular forager, you'll know that these resilient splashes of sunshine are a valuable asset. If not, prepare to be amazed. Either way, it's all great. The good news for the dandies is that we humans are learning to love them; for many years, they were just a nuisance to mow or strim over and over and over in the spring, summer and even into the autumn months, with piles of them consigned with the grass to the compost bin.

An initiative with wildlife at its heart that closely affects dandelions is "No Mow May". This was started in 2019 by Plantlife, a conservation charity in the UK. The idea is simple. Mow your grass all you like, except not in May. As I mentioned earlier, we in Britain have lost some 97 per cent of our former flower-rich meadows since the 1930s; it's worth repeating this as the loss is pretty shocking when you think about it. However, No Mow May highlights how even the smallest grassy patch, when we work together, will make a significant difference to nature, people and the planet. Hoorah for the dandelions!

HOW TO IDENTIFY DANDELION

Dandelions are easy to recognize, even for those who think they can't tell a plant from a pie dish. In the unlikely event that you don't know what they look like, look for the bright yellow flowerheads that are actually made up of multiple flowers and the deeply lobed leaves (which inspire the French name *dents-de-lion* – "lion's teeth") growing in a basal rosette. The flowerheads are around from March to October, turning to fluffy white seedheads like puffballs.

ALL ABOUT DANDELION

A single dandelion plant can produce over 5,000 seeds a year, travelling up to 8km (5 miles) in the wind, not forgetting that the wispy parachutes can also hitch a lift on our clothes, in the car, on horseback and more. The seedheads lend themselves to fun for kids (blowing dandelion clocks to make wishes, etc.), which we all know about.

Dandelions' history is as deep as their roots (which go down some 4.5m (15ft) and, moreover, clone when they are divided); the Romans, Greeks, Chinese and more admired the plant for its beauty as well as its medicinal uses. The leaves have been known for centuries as a diuretic; one of its French names is *pissenlit*, which you can probably work out for yourself. Dandelion is also considered detoxifying, used in multiple ways from treating a hangover to help acne and eczema.

Dandelions have more vitamin A than spinach, more vitamin C than tomatoes, and contain iron, calcium and potassium too.

How to Eat a Dandelion

Make sure you forage the dandelion from an environment free of contaminants. The flavour is not to everyone's taste, as we are generally not used to such wildness. Some love it, others not so much. Try the leaves chopped and wilted with other fresh leaves, oven-roasted garlic cloves, melted butter or oil and seasoning to taste, as a side dish. The petals are fun to use in cupcakes, and dandelion tea, made with the petals, is surprisingly sweet so long as you pick the flowers in full sun rather than when the rain has washed away the pollen.

2. Burdock

(Arctium lappa)

In the same family as dandelion (Asteraceae) comes the burdock, and this pairing is possibly one of the most extraordinarily delicious in wild food. Plant names of burdock are numerous, a nod to its importance over the thousands or millions of years that it has been on the planet, and include beggars' buttons, thorny burr, gobo (Japanese) and "happy major", this last added to the collection by Maud Grieve, who wrote the incredibly useful *A Modern Herbal* (1931), the very epitome of herbal lore. (If you find this book in a charity store at a decent price, buy it. Don't worry if your children are hungry and you just lost your job.)

HOW TO IDENTIFY BURDOCK

Burdock can grow to a height of 1.5m (5ft). Initially, the plant will have a set of leaves, some smaller, some larger, flattish to the ground, with a wavy appearance. As the plant grows, the purple thistle-like flowerheads emerge on long stamens, the tiny hooks ready for action. These then become the brown seedheads that stick and cling to the fur and clothes of passing animals and humans. It's worth having a close look at these hooks, which are a work of art unto themselves.

ALL ABOUT BURDOCK

Did you know that the first moon landings happened because of burdock?! George de Mestral, a Swiss engineer, was out walking his dog one day in 1941, thinking about how he might be able to make a better fastening for one of his wife's dresses. As he thought, his dog, Milka, emerged from the bushes, covered in burrs. Rather than simply clip away those burrs,

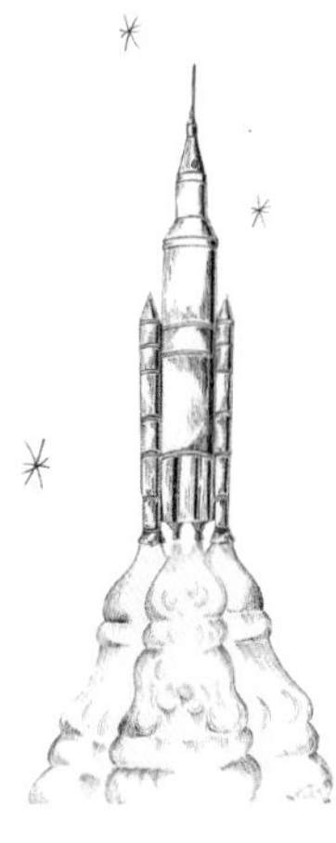

Mistral had a good look at them, presumably with a magnifying glass. He realized that each and every seed burr had a little hook, which he found a way to emulate using nylon threads. He patented the idea as *velcro* in 1955, and subsequently the patent was used by NASA, who were looking for a way to stop things floating around the gravity-free environment of a spaceship.

Like dandelion, burdock is known in herbal medicine for its detoxifying powers. It was traditionally used for kidney stones – Culpeper wrote that, "The seed is much commended to break the stone and cause it to be expelled by urine" – and also for fevers and gout.

Dandelion and Burdock Cordial

Serve this delicious foraged cordial with tonic or fizzy water for a refreshing pick-me-up, or add boiling water for a comforting bedtime tea.

You will need:

3 tbsp dandelion root, fresh or dried, cleaned thoroughly
3 tbsp burdock root, fresh or dried, cleaned thoroughly
6cm/2½in fresh ginger root, chopped roughly
3 star anise, crushed (the bottom of a mortar is a good tool)
250g/9oz dark muscovado sugar

1. Add the roots, ginger and star anise to a large saucepan with 800ml/28fl oz/scant 3½ cups water, bring gently to the boil and simmer on a medium heat until the roots have infused and the water is a dark brown colour – between 30 and 45 minutes.

2. Leave to cool a little, then strain through a fine-meshed sieve or muslin (I often use both).

3. Return the liquid to the pan and add the sugar, heating until it has dissolved and the liquid thickens into a syrupy texture. Keep refrigerated in clean, sterilized screw-top bottles.

3. Cleavers

(Galium aparine)

This little plant belongs to the Rubiaceae family and, you might be surprised to hear, is a cousin of both chinchona (used to make quinine) and the coffee plant. *Galium* comes from the Greek word for "milk", as the flowers were, once upon a time, used to curdle milk in the cheese-making process. *Aparine* means "to cling" or "seize". Common names for this plant include catchweed, goosegrass, hitchhikers, stickyweed, stickyjack . . . the list runs on.

HOW TO IDENTIFY CLEAVERS

This gorgeous, clinging creature, with long stems and tiny, white four-petalled flowers, is covered in little hooks that make it "sticky". It will climb as high as it can, up bushes and garden sheds, to the annoyance of many a gardener who might not know that it is to be treasured.

Depending on where you are in the world, cleavers are available even in the winter months. Here in Wales, I've noticed that young plants grow all the time unless there's severe snow, which is a rarity. However, as with many of our plant friends, cleavers are at their best when young, emerging in the springtime (just like us), yawning awake from the fug of winter.

ALL ABOUT CLEAVERS

This unassuming plant is valued for its blood cleansing and diuretic effect, purifying and getting rid of stagnancy and sluggishness. All parts of this plant can be used; there are many different ways of using cleavers, the easiest being to pop into a water bottle (a see-through one is nice) with a squeeze of lemon or lime to taste. Sip during the course of the day and tell me you don't feel better for it.

Otherwise, use it as a sparky addition to early spring salads to get the benefit of that impressive juicy lymphatic goodness. And don't boil or even heat this plant – it is tender.

Cleavers seeds start to appear in the late summer or early autumn; don't eat them raw as the fine hairs that you see will be an irritant. What you can do with the seeds (which look like nothing so much as a pair of tiny testicles, possibly belonging to a fairy) is make a decent coffee substitute, if you have the time and inclination to do so. Harvest a good load of the seeds and roast in a low oven, then grind in a coffee grinder.

I have a personal story to tell you. I don't want to go on and on about cancer, but this one is a good one. I like cleavers; aside from their medicinal use, they are really pretty, with an optimistic outlook. I have used them in water bottles (as mentioned) for several years. During my cancer treatment, I was told by the nurse in the hospital that I would certainly need lymph node drainage. As you might imagine, this was devastating; I wanted, at least, to be able to do *something* useful and I had thought that the cleavers, which are known in herbal medicine for their detoxifying qualities and for relieving swollen lymph glands, would be my ally. And indeed, after much further drinking of cleavers-infused water, when the time came for the scan, guess what? The lymph nodes were squeaky clean!

Thank you, cleavers. Often, plants get things right on the nail. I can't actually tell you just how happy I was to know that this plant was truly an incredible friend to me. With their help, I was fearless.

4. Coltsfoot

(Tussilago farfara)

This lovely plant is often mistaken for its cousin, the dandelion (see pages 209–210). Its commonest folk name came about because the leaves do look a little like a foal's foot – with a squint, perhaps. Other folk names include son-before-father (because it flowers before the leaves appear), foal's foot, tushies, baccy plant and coughwort. You might also see the plant named as bechie, a derivation of the Greek word for "cough". Tussilago came from the Latin *tussis*, which means "cough", while *ago* means "act", revealing its traditional medicinal use. (I also think that *Tussilago farfara*, possibly one of my favourite botanical names, would make a great stage name for a dancer at the Folies Bergère.) This plant is widespread in many areas of the world, and is happy to plant itself in stony soil.

HOW TO IDENTIFY COLTSFOOT

It looks similar to dandelion, with yellow daisy-like flowers and fluffy seedheads. Signs that tell you that this is *not* a dandelion are the oddly fleshy scales that cover the stem (a dandy has a smooth stem). The scaly stems have a pinkish flush, and the leaves have a sort of scalloped heart shape. Also, if you are observant, you might notice that the flowers appear prior to the leaves. The underside of the young herb forms a film that can be rubbed away to reveal a shiny leaf, a distinct means of recognition for the plant, providing many happy minutes in rubbing the film from the shiny part.

***SAFETY:* This is one to avoid during pregnancy and breastfeeding. Do not use if you have a history of liver disease, as the research has shown that the plant contains pyrrolizidine alkaloids that may build up to cause liver damage. Do not consume the flowers. Consult a medical herbalist before use.**

ALL ABOUT COLTSFOOT

According to tradition, you can also use this shiny new leaf, once the film has been peeled away, as a "mirror" for fortune telling. Unfortunately, the details of the divination charm seem to have faded from our collective memories. Never mind. You could make it up!

The fluffy seedheads were once upon a time used to stuff pillows; if you think that this would have been a time-consuming venture, then I would hazard a guess that you would be correct.

Not so long ago, the part of the world where I live, Wales, was renowned for coal mining, a hazardous, relentless and gruelling endeavour, especially in the conditions of earlier centuries when the miners worked long hours, up to 12 hours a day, with just one day (Sunday) free. The mines were dank, the miners unable to stand up, and even children were sent down in the pursuit of the "black gold". What has this to do with coltsfoot, you might ask? In my foraging life, I'm always scanning for plants, working out how they might have travelled somewhere, what conditions they need, what they are (or were) used for. And I have noticed that coltsfoot is often found where there were mines or, more specifically, miners.

Coltsfoot has long been used for throat conditions and, for this reason, the miners, who suffered respiratory conditions, would smoke it as a tobacco. The presence of coltsfoot tells me that there are probably mines nearby. Nine times out of ten, I am right. The plant would have been stored in pockets and shaken out on the ground, where the seeds could germinate. The miners would not have had to go far to find a soothing smoke.

Pliny the Elder, the Roman polymath, also smoked coltsfoot. It is said that he used a hollow reed as a pipe. Coltsfoot is still used in herbal medicine as an expectorant and for a tickly cough.

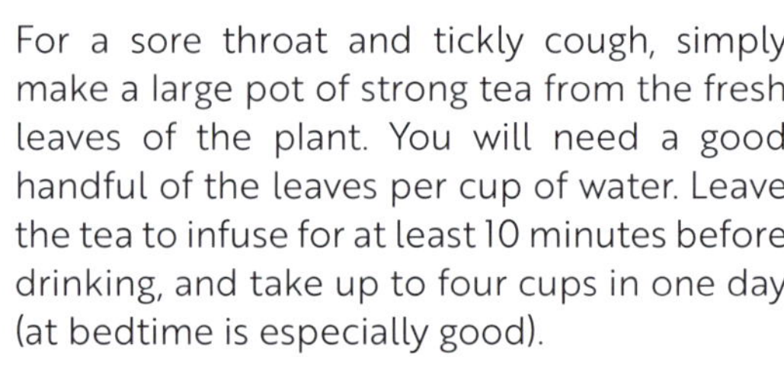

For a sore throat and tickly cough, simply make a large pot of strong tea from the fresh leaves of the plant. You will need a good handful of the leaves per cup of water. Leave the tea to infuse for at least 10 minutes before drinking, and take up to four cups in one day (at bedtime is especially good).

5. Self-heal

(Prunella vulgaris)

This perennial plant is found in temperate climates. Pretty little self-heal is so common that it is often unnoticed, but if you do get to look closely at this diminutive plant, you will see that it is as gorgeous as any orchid. Other names include all heal, heal all, heart of the earth, blue curls, slough heal, woundwort and carpenter's herb.

HOW TO IDENTIFY SELF-HEAL

Self-heal is a member of the mint family (Lamiaceae); look for the tell-tale square stems. This little plant has more than a passing resemblance to betony (see pages 24–25), but that is to be expected given that they are cousins. The narrow leaves that arch back from the rigid stem and grow in opposite pairs are a good giveaway for both herbs. Flowers grow in dense clusters at the top of stems, in colours ranging through pink, blue and purple. The flower has an orchid-like "tongue" that looks in profile a little like a hook, hence the folk names hook heal or hook herb.

Self-heal can be found in meadows and grasslands, on wasteland, at the edges of woodlands and frequently on lawns, but only if they are allowed to grow rather than being mowed down at the drop of a hat.

ALL ABOUT SELF-HEAL

Prunella has been used in Chinese herbal medicine for over 2,000 years, specifically for the liver. The Chinese name for the plant is translated as "summer dry herb". Only the flower spikes are used in Chinese herbal medicine, considered to be cooling for the liver. A way of knowing if the remedy is working is the brightening of previously dull eyes.

In the West, self-heal is useful for any kind of bleeding (hence its name carpenter's herb), including heavy periods, as well as for routine cuts and grazes; the whole plant can be washed, crushed and used as a poultice. It is used as a remedy for swollen glands. According to the Doctrine of Signatures, the way the flower lolls open suggests the mouth and throat. Many of the ailments that we suffer from today have been problematic for centuries, as we find from an herbal written by John Parkinson, a botanist and herbalist who died in 1650. He recommends that the juice of self-heal, mixed with "honey of roses", as a remedy for "all ulcers and sores in the mouth and throat, and those also in the secret parts". Some things never change.

This plant is edible. Traditionally the use is to dry the whole plant, make into powder and use as a tea, but to be honest it's just as easy to pour boiling water over two or three of the flowers (make sure there are no insects about to be accidentally boiled), add honey if you wish, cool a little and drink. To use the herb through the year, dry the whole plant, shake the seeds onto your garden and use the rest as needed. A cold infusion is said to be good for menopausal flushes, and a tea is good for feverish conditions, mouth ulcers and throat problems, among others.

6. St John's Wort

(Hypericum perforatum)

You might not realize that there are several different plants that have historically gone by the name of St John's wort because they flower around the feast day of St John the Baptist (24 June). They include oxeye daisies (see pages 188–190), chamomile (see pages 26–28), common mugwort (see pages 14–16) and chrysanthemum. Perforate St John's wort, however, is the plant that is generally thought of as *numero uno* of St John's worts, just as mugwort is foremost among the nine herbs of the original spell.

Before this plant was ascribed to the saint, it was named by the ancient Greeks using two separate words translating as "over" (hyper) and "image" (icon). This was because the plant was hung over the statues of the gods, to ward off malicious spirits. If you like, *hypericum* was a sort of magical mirror that could absorb and dispel evil entities. *Hypericum* is named in numerous languages, as you might imagine, and has numerous folk names: penny John, rose of Sharon, touch-and-heal and many others.

HOW TO IDENTIFY ST JOHN'S WORT

Indigenous to Europe, northern Africa and western Asia, *Hypericum perforatum* grows in dry, grassy places as well as in meadows, wasteland and verges. Most recently, while I was on the top deck of a bus, I noticed a stand of them, down below, looking as though they were waiting for the next bus to come along.

To see for yourself the magical wonder of St John's wort, you need a bright summer's day, around about the same time as St John's Day. Hold one of its leaves to the sun, and you will see many tiny, perforated dots. Squeeze the plant between your fingers and you will reveal the "blood" of John the Baptist, from whom it was supposed to have originated. The plant usually grows 30–75cm (12–30in) high, with star-shaped, five-petalled yellow flowers on smooth reddish stems.

ALL ABOUT ST JOHN'S WORT

In exploring these herbs (and others), we need to be time travellers of great imagination. Prior to Christianity, the red juice that emerged from the plant was the blood of Balder, the Germanic god of nature, light and the summer. Alternatively, it might be the blood of Odin, who was wounded by a wild boar. The summer solstice is, like its opposing festival at midwinter, a time of bright fires and feasts.

The blood-red oil made from perforate St John's wort was regarded as a magical potion; for example, for warding off witches or as protection against rabid dogs. Paracelsus (1493–1541), the rather eccentric physician and alchemist, believed that the tiny dots on the plant would drive away ghosts. The Devil also stakes his claim on this little plant. Because he was so jealous of such an effective but tiny flower, one night, so the story goes, he perforated all the leaves. But the plan failed, the plant kept its magical properties and can even be used to drive the Devil away.

One of the best-known uses of St John's wort was in warding off evil spirits, and those who were known to be "mad" or "insane" were given an infusion to cure them. These days we know that the herb is a useful antidepressant. Perforate St John's wort is used as a restorative for the nervous system, and also by some to ease menstrual tension and some kinds of period pain. In cases like these, it is advisable to seek the help of a reputable herbalist. These little yellow flowers pack a heavy punch, so treat them with respect.

7. Bramble

(Rubus fruticosus)

As foraging goes, I notice time and again how certain plants are passed over for more exotic specimens. The bramble – also known as the blackberry, for its fruit – is a good example. When I ask a group which plants people already know, the bramble is often forgotten. Another case of looking but not seeing. However, the might of this humble plant might well surprise you.

We don't know how old the bramble is, but we know that it has been growing wild in numerous places around much of the globe. Folk names include black heg, brambleberry and scaldberries.

HOW TO IDENTIFY BRAMBLE

You would think that, in most places, people would know this plant, and you would be right, but I have also found people that know it but haven't tried it. Strictly speaking, the bramble is a thorny thicket, which grows just about anywhere and can grow so rapidly that gathering the fruits can become hazardous without gloves. Clusters of white or pink flowers are followed by the appearance of the fruits made up of many tiny individual fruits – the blackberries. Although they traditionally fruit in late summer/early autumn, having gathered the berries over many years, I have noted that in some places they are out a few weeks earlier than they used to be.

ALL ABOUT BRAMBLE

In the Celtic tradition, the fruits were sacred to Brigid, goddess of poetry, healing and smithing. It is said, however, that eating blackberries after Old Michaelmas Day (11 October) is bad practice. The story goes that the Devil fell into a bramble thicket and left his curse on the thorny plant.

We don't see whooping cough often these days, but not so long ago it was common. A remedy for this was to pass the poor child under a natural bramble arch three times before breakfast, while facing the rising sun, for nine successive days.

My partner, who is Irish, tells me that the old Brehon laws about shrubs and trees named bramble as one of the "bushes of the woods", meaning that the unlawful clearing of a thicket would result in a fine.

Blackberries are packed with vitamins and minerals, including vitamin C. All blackberry-like fruits contain antioxidants called anthocyanins, including elderberry. The leaves, as well as the fruits, of blackberry are good for us; the tannin has a similar effect to a green tea, good for mouth ulcers and gum disease. Cooled, the tea can be used on the skin, the tannins tightening the face as a skin lotion.

Happily at home in the grottiest of wastelands, the bramble is a sociable plant, offering its berries to you to gather for a delicious crumble, a cheap treat with ice cream or custard. Some time ago, trawling TK Maxx, I found a gadget for removing the pips from berries. I had lots of blackberries so I tried my new toy. The loss of the pips made the fruit taste even better, giving it a silky texture and a flavour a little like vanilla.

An Invocation to Heal Scalds

Blackberries were used in spells to gain riches; perhaps because of the abundance of the berries. The plant was used to heal scalds, by dipping nine blackberry leaves in clear spring water and then laying them against the wound, chanting the following 27 times (three times to each leaf):

"Three ladies came from the east
One with fire and two with frost
Out with fire, in with frost."

This is an ancient invocation to the goddess Brigid.

8. Rosebay Willowherb

(Chamaenerion angustifolium & Epilobium angustifolium)

There are almost 200 plants in the genus *Epilobium*. It is likely you will have seen them in wasteland, or in a busy city. You might spot them next to meadowsweet (see pages 88–89). The 200 or so willowherbs include tall willowherb (*Epilobium brachycarpum*), pale willowherb (*Epilobium roseum*), American willowherb (*Epilobium ciliatum*), pygmy willowherb (*Epilobium pygmaeum)* and even an Olympic Mountain willowherb (*Epilobium mirabile*). In this case, we are looking at the rosebay willowherb, *Chamaenerion angustifolium* or *Epilobium angustifolium*. An easier name to remember is fireweed, an apt one, as you will see.

HOW TO IDENTIFY ROSEBAY WILLOWHERB

The "willow" part of the name is a clue. The leaves are much like those of a willow, long and narrow. Rosebay willowherb's pink flowers grow at the end of the stem, while other willowherbs may have more compact paired clusters of flowers, and its leaves grow spirally on the stem in contrast to the paired arrangement of others in the genus. When they are ready to set seed in summer or autumn, willowherbs produce fluffy plumes, which help to disperse seeds.

ALL ABOUT ROSEBAY WILLOWHERB

Richard Mabey says that John Gerard (16th-century herbalist, botanist and gardener) knew the plant as a rare woodland being and managed to find, and grow, the seeds. However, with the coming of the railways, rosebay willowherb began to branch out into a wider world. When large areas of woodland were felled during World War I, the plant erupted; it's possible the seeds had been in the soil for millennia. It was noted that wherever there was fire, rosebay willowherb proliferated, first as the bright pink and purple outliers, then as gossamer clouds of drifting seeds.

Now, it is safe to say, most gardeners see willowherb as a nuisance, and even I can empathize with this. The stands of tall flowers do have a self-satisfied air, as though they know how annoying they can be. They make dogs and horses sneeze (and humans, too). We dig them up, only to find that they pop up in greater numbers than the year before. The seeds stick to washing, and even invade greenhouses when no one is looking.

But for all this, for some reason rosebay willowherb makes me smile. It is so beautiful; use a magnifying glass to see some of the delicate seed strands and the tiny flowers of the smaller plants. And, of course, it has its medicinal uses. The fresh leaves can be used like a poultice, to help minor wounds to heal. Simply mash with a bandage and use as needed. A syrup made of the leaves and petals, with added honey and hot water, cooled to touch, is used for diarrhoea.

Rosebay Willowherb Tea

To make rosebay willowherb tea, start by stripping the leaves from the plant, then stripping them from the stems. Roll handfuls of them between the palms until they darken in colour, then leave the rolled-up leaves covered with a dish towel overnight or longer. This allows them to ferment (just like any good premium tea).

When the smell gets sweeter, just like fermented grass, it's time for them to be dried. If you have a dehydrator, great; if not, dry out in your oven on the lowest setting with the door open or simply leave them in the sunshine, turning regularly. When dried, keep them in an airtight tin, otherwise they can go mouldy. You can now use the leaves to make your tea!

9. Docks

(Rumex spp.)

Everyone knows what a dock is, right? Kids run to find them if they get stung by a nettle. They like to grow everywhere, and have been used for at least 2,000 years. A member of the Polygonaceae family, there are some 200 different *Rumex* species (at least). Generations of farmers have waged battle with them, as the tap roots like to dig themselves deep into the ground, producing leaves that take light and nutrition from other species. Those roots are like 10th-century Crusaders using swords and maces, but faced with our bombs and drones (our toxic chemicals), the docks have no chance in the long run.

There are lots of different docks to play with, which were often named for the uses that they were put to. For example, the larger leaves of butter dock (also known as common dock, broadleaved dock, wayside dock or *Rumex obtusifolius*), were used to keep butter cool for the market. Curled dock, aka yellow dock or *Rumex crispus*, like others in the family, was at one time used as a cure for jaundice, a disease that causes the skin or whites of the eyes to turn yellow.

HOW TO IDENTIFY DOCK

Dock is recognized by its oval leaves, with a pronounced rib down the middle, growing in rosettes, and the flower spikes that turn into reddish-brown seedheads. The leaves of common dock are more heart-shaped with smooth, flat edges, while curled dock has narrower, lance-shaped leaves with wavy edges. The largest of the family is the great water dock, which reaches a height of 1.5–1.8m/5–6ft, and is most often seen along the banks of a river, but seems to be rare these days.

ALL ABOUT DOCK

If you like rhubarb, this plant is also a dock; the astringent quality of all docks matches the sour garden plant, which generally divides people who love it from those who don't! If you have never tasted a dock, the best thing to do is to find sorrel (*Rumex acetosa*), a member of the same family. It can be identified by the arrow-shaped leaf with a "nick", and, if you look closely, there's a distinct sparkle going on in the leaf too. Of all the dock family, this is the most palatable. Sorrel is also called sallies, after the salicylic acid that gives the mouth-puckering flavour, exactly like a crisp Granny Smith apple.

Dock seeds are edible, used to flavour fish, for example, or simply there to nibble on during a walk. They can also be used to make a "porridge"; I have tried this and found it not to my taste, but you might love it. Only one way to find out!

This next story circles back to this chapter's introduction and tells a tale of refugees, plants and the people who love them.

Sometimes, even when we think that we are alert and open and clever, we miss something that is so obvious. This is exactly what happened to me when I was volunteering with a large group of refugees, taking them foraging at Craig-y-Nos, a beautiful country park in the grounds of a castle that was once the home of opera singer Adelina Patti (1843–1919), the Madonna of her day.

When I take out refugee foraging groups, I don't always know where everyone comes from, or what has happened to them and their families. And it is bewildering, the numbers of people that need support. But these foraging days are generally happy ones.

One of the volunteer group came to find me, with a request from one particular woman, who I think was Kurdish. The love of plants brought us together, and I understood that she was looking for something, describing with her hands something tallish; the only thing I could think to do was to stake out the entire park to see if she could find what she needed. There was still some wild garlic around, so she gathered some of it, but it was clear that this wasn't what she was looking for. Dandelion? No. She shook her head. She knew it, but it wasn't what she wanted. Elder? Yes, but no. Tiny little strawberries? She gathered lots of those and we ate them immediately, laughing . . . Mallow? Not that. And then, when I thought I'd failed, we rounded a corner and there they were. A large patch of docks. Aha! This was what she wanted. I helped her fill the plastic bag; we used a mushroom knife to cut the docks more easily (they can be hellishly hard to get out of the soil) and, finding another bag, we filled that too.

What was she going to do with them? She showed me, taking a large leaf and rolling it. "Dolma", she said, holding out the docks. She would steam them, add other ingredients such as fish or potatoes, and serve them to her two kids, teenagers who had come on the foraging day too.

We walked back to base, where the refugee group were busy making food for us all to share, and one of the party told me that my new friend had no idea where her mother and father were, or her husband; his phone was dead. As we went to go, she hugged me, and then shook the precious weeds in her bag.

"Home", she said, with a huge smile.

I didn't know if this meant that she was going home, or that the docks reminded her of home. I like to imagine the latter. Maybe both? Afterwards, I tried to find the lady again, but this was not possible. I'd love to know how she is . . . and where.

Dock Dolma

This recipe was given to me by one of the volunteers who took part in the day. If, on your first try, your dock dolmas fall apart, don't worry. They will still be delicious!

You will need:

250g/9oz young dock leaves (*Rumex obtusifolius*), cleaned, with extra leaves to layer the pan
50g/1¾oz pine kernels or chopped nuts of choice
150g/5½oz long-grain rice, soaked, rinsed and drained
275g/10oz onions, finely chopped
3–4 spring onions/scallions, finely chopped
3 tbsp each of chopped fresh mint, dill, oregano and parsley
2–3 garlic cloves, finely chopped
150ml/5fl oz/⅔ cup olive oil
1 lemon, juiced, plus extra lemon juice to serve
Salt and black pepper
Plain yogurt, to serve

1. Blanch the dock leaves in boiling salted water for about a minute to make them softer, then remove with a slotted spoon, drain and pat dry.

2. Lightly toast the pine kernels or nuts in a dry frying pan.

3. In a large bowl, combine the toasted pine nuts with the rice, onions, spring onions, herbs and garlic. Add half the oil and half the lemon juice.

4. Line the bottom of a large sauté pan or saucepan (with an accompanying lid) with the extra dock leaves.

5. Spread out a blanched dock leaf, even side up, and place 1 teaspoon of stuffing on the leaf.

6. Carefully fold over the edges of the leaf to make a parcel. This is the trickiest part!

7. Repeat with the rest of the stuffing and leaves.

8. Arrange the stuffing parcels tightly in the pan, with the loose ends tucked underneath.

9. Pour over the rest of the oil and lemon juice, and season with salt and pepper.

10. Put an inverted plate (slightly smaller than the pan) on top of the dolmas, to keep them in place.

11. Pour over 300ml/10½fl oz/1¼ cups water, cover the pan with the lid and cook gently for 50 minutes.

12. Serve hot or cold, with the lemon juice or plain yoghurt.

Forager's Choice by Lucia Stuart

When my first foraging book (*The Hedgerow Handbook*) was published, I asked my friend Lucia Stuart, owner of the Wild Kitchen in Deal, which offers foraging and feasting experiences in Kent, if she might let me have a recipe. And, oh my, what a recipe – for Elderflower and Rhubarb Ripple Ice Cream! And now she has let me have another humdinger; thanks, Lucia!

Lucia's Rosehip and Dock Seed Scones

These scones are versatile and can be eaten with a sweet or savoury filling. Forage the dock seeds on a dry day at the end of summer (ask a professional forager to help you identify the seeds). Shake the plants to remove insects and dust, then rub them off the stem. They will store for 12 months in an airtight container. Dock seeds contain fibre and iron, hence the red colour. The hips of *Rosa rugosa* or beach rose are similar to cherry tomatoes in size. Forage them when they are ripe, soft and sweet at the end of the season. Cut each one in half to remove and discard the seeds, hairs and calyx before use.

You will need:
225g/8oz plain/all-purpose flour, preferably organic, plus extra for dusting
6 tbsp dock seeds
1 tbsp baking powder
1 tsp salt
1 teacupful of *Rosa rugosa* hips, very fresh and very ripe
40g/1½oz unsalted butter, cold and cubed
150ml/5fl oz/scant ⅔ cup cold whole milk

1. Preheat the oven to 220°C/425°F/gas mark 7.

2. In a bowl mix the flour, dock seeds, baking powder and salt. Add a teacupful of ripe *Rosa rugosa* hips.

3. Using your fingertips, rub the cold butter into the flour until it resembles breadcrumbs, stir in the milk with a metal spoon. The dough must be cold, moist and soft but not sticky.

4. With floured hands, tip onto a floured surface and fold over to incorporate air – handle gently! Roll it out gently until 2.5cm/1in thick.

5. Use a high-topped scone cutter to quickly cut out the scones. Place on a greased baking sheet.

6. Bake for 5 minutes, then bake for a further 5–10 minutes at 180°C/350°F/gas mark 4 until golden and light. If overcooked they will become dry.

Acknowledgements & Resources

First, let me say thank you to you for reading this book.

At the time of writing, the world is going through a terrifying time, something that is bizarre and disgraceful and unnecessary. But I suspect that you, like me, believe that most of us are reasonable, caring and courageous. Do what you can to make your own patch of this beautiful world safe and stay as strong as you can. Be inspired by the nine cunning herbs that are free. Make a difference! Think how you can help this beautiful planet and meet like-minded people at the same time.

Here are some thank yous to the books, organizations and people that enabled this book to become a real, living entity.

BOOKS

Thank you to:

Ash, R. et al, *Folklore, Myths and Legends of Britain* (Reader's Digest, 1973)

Baker, M. *Discovering the Folklore of Plants* (Shire Publications, 2008)

Bishop, C., *The Book of Home Remedies and Herbal Cures* (Octopus, 1979)

Blair, K., *The Wild Wisdom of Weeds* (Chelsea Green Publishing, 2014)

Callendar, R., *What Remains* (Chelsea Green Publishing, 2022)

de Cleene, M. and Lejeune, M.C., *Compendium of Symbolic and Ritual Plants in Europe: I Trees & Shrubs; II Herbs* (Mens & Cultuur Uitgevers N.V., 2003)

Conway, P., *Tree Medicine* (Piatkus, 2001)

Cooper, Q. and Sullivan, P., *Maypole, Martyrs and Mayhem* (Bloomsbury, 1994)

Culpeper, N., *Culpeper's Complete Herbal* (Wordsworth Reference, 1995)

Deakin, R., *Wildwood* (Penguin Books, 2008)

Evelyn, J., Masson, M. et al, *The Grand Salad from John Evelyn's Aceteria* (Longman, 1986)

Gibbons, E. *Stalking the Wild Asparagus* (Hood and Co, 1962)

Graves, R., *The Greek Myths* (Folio Society, 1996)

Grieve, Mrs M., (edited and introduced by Leyel, Mrs C.F.), *A Modern Herbal* (Tiger Books, 1996)

Harvey, G., *The Handbook of Contemporary Animism* (Acumen, 2013)

Hatfield, A.W., *How To Enjoy Your Weeds* (Frederick Muller, 1969)

Hoffman, D., *Welsh Herbal Medicine* (Abercastle Publications, Dinefwr Press, 1999)

Hopkins, J.S., with Baudey, R., Wilder, A. , Lund, J.A. and Cudmore, D, *The Nine Plants Spell* (Hyldyr, 2024)

Lerner, R., *Dandelion Hunter* (Lyons Press, 2013)

Mabey, R., *Weeds* (Profile Books, 2020)

Mac Coitir, N., *Ireland's Wild Plants* (The Collins Press, 2016)

Moerman, D., *Native American Ethnobotany* (Timber Press, 1998)

Paine, A., *Healing Plants of the Celtic Druids* (John Hunt Publishing, 2017)

Peterson, L.A., *Edible Wild Plants of Eastern/Central North America* (Houghton Mifflin, 1978)

Rogers, R.D., *Worms, Worts and Leeches* (Prairie Deva Press, 2018)

Seed Sistas, The, *The Sensory Herbal Handbook* (Watkins Publishing, 2019)

ORGANIZATIONS

Thank you to:

Brooklyn Botanic Garden www.bbg.org, for information on shepherd's purse.

National Center for Complementary and Integrative Health www.nccih.nih.gov, for information on evening primrose oil.

www.brainfacts.org, for information on how our sense of smell works.

Spurn Point Visitor Centre, Yorkshire.

The Association of Lighthouse Keepers in both the UK and USA. All the Keepers are retired now, the last lighthouse in the UK automated in 1998 – there are stories primed for someone to write, sooner rather than later.

The Woodland Classroom, for info about how to harvest sea buckthorn.

The Wildlife Trust, for information regarding the plight of meadows. Also thanks to the Save the Meadows coalition in FDR Park, and others like it around the planet.

Everyone who loves trees (that is, all of us) and, in particular, the Woodland Trust, the Tree Council, Stump Up For Trees, and, in the USA, One Tree Planted, the Arbor Day Foundation, Trees for Cities, and many more. Please excuse me telling you about the closest tree-related organization to me, the Brecon Beacons National Park, which is also a Dark Skies Reserve. These places are incredible and need to be cherished. What would the skies look like if they were polluted with space debris?

In the UK, the Wildlife and Wetlands Trust (WWT, the wetlands restoration charity) and the RSPB. In the USA, Ducks Unlimited, Wetlands and Stream Conservation, and the North American Wetlands Conservation.

Incredible Edibles. This organization is inspiring and their roots spread far and wide; see the maps to find like-minded people in your area with whom to share abundance!

The Association of Foragers. Founded by a small group, spearheaded by Andy Hamilton and a few others, this organization has gone from strength to strength, with initiatives such as the Wildbiome Project (the brainchild of Monica Wild), which seeks to find out how wild food can work to our advantage (or otherwise) by encouraging members to eat only wild food (including plants, fish, roadkill, etc.) for a certain period and monitoring what happens to the gut biome during that time. If you would like to join the association, you will find information online at foragers-association.org. If you are looking for a forager, the best bet will be to find one local to you. Rates vary depending on what you need.

Thanks also to the Herb Society, whose members are always helpful. Founded in 1927 by Hilda Leyel as the Society of Herbalists, their aims are "to increase the understanding and use of herbs for health and wellbeing, provide information, knowledge and news on all aspects of herbs, bring together all those with an interest in herbs, from the amateur to the professional, and to provide a worldwide forum for the exchange of ideas and information."
Do have a look at @herbsociety.org.uk

PEOPLE

Thank you to the nine other foragers who have contributed to this book. In no particular order, they are:

Lady Danni Morinich @ladydanni
Julia Horton-Mansfield @reallywildemporium
Chloé of Gourmet Gatherings @gourmetgatherings
Lucia Stuart @luciathewildkitchen
Daniel Butler @fungiforays
Rob Gould @cotswoldforager
Natasha Lloyd @gathering.nature
Andy Hamilton @theotherandyhamilton
Sam Webster @foragingforages

Thank you to J.S. Hopkins for permission to quote from the *Nine Plants Spell.*

Thank you Alan Bergo aka @foragerchef for the info about how to safely eat thistles!

Thank you to Kate Unwin @themoonandthefurrow, who lives and breathes the old ways in an authentic and heartfelt way. This is a very inspiring person.

A big thank you to Andy and Kate at Urban Herbs, always up for a challenge. Thanks, both, for hunting down unusual ingredients for the rare 15 Herbs Charm; we are still nonplussed as to what it does!

Thank you to all of you who prefer an active and useful garden – best for insects, diversity, imagination, colour, beauty and also sharing!

Thank you to the people who make the music that helps me to think, write and generally be happy. When I was writing this book, I started out listening to fairly random tracks, but soon I realized that Hildegarde of Bingen was the best match for this particular book, as her music straddles the ages and fits perfectly with the plants, the stories and the moments when I thought I was going ever so quietly mad. You might also enjoy the Spotify playlist entitled "The Tree Forager", which I created to accompany my book of that name.

A huge thanks is due to Helen Nicholson, who drew the beautiful images that grace this book.Also I'm very grateful to designers Karen and Eleri, whose work is meticulous!

Thank you to all the team at Watkins, especially Sophie Blackman.

Above all, Fiona Robertson lifted me up when everything seemed utterly impossible. I will never forget such kindness.

INDEX OF PLANTS

ABOUT THE AUTHOR

Adele Nozedar is the author of books including *The Hedgerow Handbook, Foraging with Kids* and *The Tree Forager*. She runs her own foraging school in the Brecon Beacons and is the only forager from Wales to be in the Lonely Planet! She is an ambassador for both The Herb Society and The Slow Food Movement. She has worked with Chatsworth gardeners to future-proof their grounds in view of global warming. She has also worked with the Garden Museum for seven years as a forager and she is a regular at Hay Festival and Green Man Festival.

ABOUT THE ILLUSTRATOR

Helen Nicholson is a Sussex based illustrator, mainly working n book illustration, and specializing in creating work around the subjects of nature and folklore. She graduated from the University of Sussex in 2014, and with a Masters from Camberwell College of Arts in 2018. When not at work in her studio, she loves walking in the downs, swimming in the sea, reading and folk singing. Instagram is the best way to follow her work as it evolves on a daily basis.

instagram.com/helennicholson_illustration

Website: helennicholson.co.uk

PRAISE FOR *FORAGING FOR HEALING HERBS*

"Adele's writing is a missing link between the lost stories, hidden powers, and healing gifts of the wild herbs we pass by every day."

Gaz Oakley, chef and author of five books including *Plant to Plate*

"This is an unusual, personal and really quite magical book, inspired by the true stories of real people."

Lia Leendertz, gardening journalist
and author of the bestselling *Almanac* series

"In this book, Adele reminds us of the sheer magic of herbs and plants and their ability to transform us, lift our mood and elevate us. These humble but mighty beings have been known for countless generations, yet in the book their ancient magic and beauty is groundbreaking, contemporary and incredibly exciting!"

Kate and Andrew Perry, founders of Urban Herbs
and authors of *The Herb Gardening Handbook*

The Nine Plants Spell

Nine fragrant herbs of a garden

Nine shady leaves of the trees

Nine bygone herbs of the meadows

Nine secret herbs of the town

Nine plashy herbs of the wetlands

Nine bracing herbs of the sea

Nine scorned seeds of the wastelands

Nine cunning herbs that are free